M000317044

GOD'S

Miracle Work
in My Life

MILIJANA HANSEE

ISBN 978-1-63844-218-9 (paperback)
ISBN 978-1-63844-219-6 (digital)

Copyright © 2021 by Milijana Hansee

All rights reserved. No part of this publication may be reproduced, distributed, or transmitted in any form or by any means, including photocopying, recording, or other electronic or mechanical methods without the prior written permission of the publisher. For permission requests, solicit the publisher via the address below.

Christian Faith Publishing, Inc.
832 Park Avenue
Meadville, PA 16335
www.christianfaithpublishing.com

Printed in the United States of America

CONTENTS

ACKNOWLEDGMENTS

This book is dedicated to my amazing two children Jelena and Aleksandar; my three granddaughters Jasmine, Isabel, Adrijanna; and my grandson, Christian, all whom I love dearly and have the honor to call my own.

A special thank you to Christian Faith Publishing and my publication specialist, Wendy, who guided me throughout this process. They made my dream a reality. Big appreciation to my editing group, Dodie, who helped me in organizing my manuscript from the start to the end. Professional Editor and Writer Marie Valentine, along with my friend, Madison, who assisted me in editing and sharing my true-life story.

I appreciate the support I received from members and friends like Dianne from my Orthodox Church who believed in me and wanted millions of people to read my story. Father John and Father Theodore, my preachers, have taught me lessons in relying on God, forgiveness of others, and forgetting all negative moments in my lifetime. They encouraged and supported me along the way in the decision to take these steps. I took their advice to release all my past pain, bitterness, and loneliness that I held for many years. I give all the glory of my story to God. With His blessings, I was able to remember so much about my life that a lot of people would have erased from their minds. I did not think this book would be possible due to my limited English, which hampered my ability to write this story on my own. I knew in my heart that God wanted me to share this story of my challenging childhood to my adult life: living in a one-room house with nine people, without today's luxuries, the loss of my mother at a young age, multiple stepmoms, my injuries, constantly working from age five to currently, lack of nutritious food and clean water, the marriage to the wrong man, the birth of my two children, my divorce, leaving my kids behind, bringing kids out of Serbia, trying to learn English, learning to drive a car, moving to America, becoming a US citizen, and the loss of the love of my life.

In this book, I share my story. I encourage everyone to have a relationship with God, because I could not have made it this far without Him. He has led me out of suffering, showing me his love, guidance, and mercies. His help has allowed me to retain these precious memories to be able to share it with others. I am able to remember every moment and situation I was in for a reason, even the experiences I wish I'd forget. The best decision in my life was to trust our almighty God. I hope to share this book of encouragement with readers throughout the world. To all the generations who believe in the power of God: God guided my life from the moment I was born to the day He inspired me to share this story.

CHAPTER 1

Background

Time has flown by for me. I'm now fifty-eight years old. My name is Milijana, a name given to me by my godparents, which was the tradition in the country where I was born. I was born in Kosovo, which Orthodox Christians called the heart of Serbia. At that time Kosovo and Serbia was part of the former Yugoslavia.

Kosovo is a Christian land where many people lost their lives to protect the country from invasion of German Nazis, Turkish, and Bulgarian Army. Kosovo is located in the southeast part of Europe, in the heart of the Balkans. Yugoslavia was formed from six republics: Croatia, Serbia, Macedonia, Slovenia, Montenegro, Bosnia, and Herzegovina, the autonomous province of Vojvodina and the autonomous region of Kosovo-Metohija. Our never-ending president was socialist, Josip Broz Tito. He then named it the Social Federal Republic of Yugoslavia. Tito was the most respected socialist in the world. Rich people stayed rich and the poor people stayed poor under his rule. There was no middle class or way to really live. Tito was against religion and people going to church to pray. Under his rule, lots of people were killed for attending churches. He would not invest money into building churches or schools. There was no freedom of speech under his rule. Socialist rule under Tito allowed other immigrants to have their own school, language, and flag. When Tito died, most of the country lost its territory and people from war. Well-known leaders from the whole world attended his funeral.

When I was born, the population of Serbia was a little over six million people and made up of many different nationalities. Most of them are Serbian people of the Orthodox faith. They are the people who build monasteries, churches, and cathedrals, with love and passion for God. Most of them were built in Kosovo, more than any other location in Serbia. It took centuries to build holy places, and our enemies destroyed them in just a few days.

Kosovo is very fertile and rich in arable land. One can grow more than enough food to sustain themselves.

My father, Milorad, was married before my mother and had two children by his first wife, Djurka. She was not an easy woman to admire. My father married very young and unhappily at eighteen years old. He married her on the recommendation of his parents, a tradition in my country at that time. He had no knowledge of the engagement. My father was so upset that he passed out when heard he was marrying a woman he didn't know. He was pressured to marry her to satisfy his parents, not because he was in love. This arranged marriage did not last very long. It fell apart. My father was a very handsome man with dark hair and dark-brown eyes. He was charming and a leader of his village. This made my stepmom jealous and angry that his attention was not solely fixed on her. Her anger would consume her so much that she neglected their children. She soon left behind my half-brother, Veljko, and half-sister, Vera, with my grandparents. Vera was three years old, and Veljko was one when he lost his life due to sickness and malnutrition.

A couple years later, after being left by his first wife, my father began searching for his soulmate. My father met my mother, Radmila, on top of the mountain named Krtok, through a neighbor and got married right away. She stood tall, with long black hair kept in a neat braid, dark-brown eyes that he couldn't resist, and a smile so beautiful. He didn't want to upset my mother with the history of his previous wife and two children, since she grew up in the mountains, isolated and with no exposure to relationships with young men. My father walked my mother into his house. Standing there was my five-year-old sister, Vera. My mother asked, "Who is this little girl? She looks like you." My father responded, "This is my sister." My mother knew that this was not the truth. This was the first time my mother learned about Vera.

After a couple hours of conversation, he finally told her the truth. My mother was very disappointed that he had lied to her. He assured my mom that he loved her and begged for forgiveness. My mother wanted to leave him and return home. She knew that she couldn't go back to her parents, as this would shame them. Her father did not want her returning home since he had ordered her to find a man, get married, and start her own life. The remembrance of his words brought tears to her eyes… At that time, tradition was to be married by the age of eighteen to twenty-five years old. At twenty-seven, my mother would've been considered "too old" for marriage. Therefore, her father was not going to allow her to move back home.

The consequences of leaving my father were too severe, so she stayed with him. She had to learn a whole new style of living: being in the same house with eight strangers (my father, his parents, his sister, his brother and his wife, their two kids, and daughter). My uncle Milan became very bossy to her. He wanted my mom to cook and clean so that his wife would have less chores. Since she was shy, she tried to please everybody by doing what they asked. Living with new rules, a minimal amount of food, and no privacy was very hard on my mom.

In this house, I was born a year later, in the cold month of November (unsure of the date). There were no doctors or nurses. A midwife helped deliver me. There were also no medications or hospitals in reach. Because of this, my birth certificate was officially annotated in city records when the weather was feasible.

At seven months old, my parents decided to visit my maternal grandparents. As they waited at the train station with my mom holding me, a drunk man passing by sent a bottle crashing into the concrete. The bottle shattered into a hundred pieces. A shard of glass flew up and sliced my nose, just missing my eyes by the grace of God. My parents ran in horror to the closest doctor's office to have stitches put in. To this day, I still wear the scar, but I am blessed to have full vision.

My Beautiful Mother and Uncle Golub

CHAPTER 2

Mother Gets Sick

My great-aunt Milka told me stories of when my mother was younger. My mother and her cousin would walk long distances to Svinjiste to visit my mom's Aunt Todora. They had to walk through the mountains and woods and eventually cross a stream. While they were walking through the woods, my mother crossed the stream over a rotten, wooden footbridge. While she was carefully making her way across, one of the boards cracked, and she fell down into the water. The weather was freezing. My mother tried to wring out as much water from her clothes as possible. She knew that she still had a long way to travel in her cold, wet clothes. It took them a couple more hours. When they finally arrived, she did not tell her aunt about the accident for fear of embarrassment. Instead, she stayed in her damp clothes until she went to sleep. After three days at her aunt's house, they returned home. Soon after, my mother fell terribly ill. Though God helped her survive, she did not fully recover. She continued to have inflammation in her lungs. She struggled with breathing issues the rest of her life.

My sister, Grozda, was born in January 1963. Once she got home, my mother struggled with feeding my sister from the day she was born since Mom was so sick. She was not able to breastfeed regularly and had to use cow's milk when it was available. When they couldn't get milk, they resorted to using a little piece of cheese cloth with sugar cubes inside so that my sister could suck on it. She cried from hunger.

Since we had no heaters in our home, my mother suffered terribly from the cold. My father took her to the hospital six months after Grozda was born, and I was only three. She stayed there for one week after being diagnosed with pneumonia. My mother worried about us and felt that no one would take better care of us than her. So against the doctor's advice, my mother came home to take care of us and nurse my sister.

The doctor tried to talk my mom into staying. She had water in her lungs that needed to be removed. She convinced the doctor that she would sign some papers, promising not to sue. On the way out of hospital, the doctor warned her that she would not survive a week.

After one week of my mom being home and living in a cold room, the doctor's words proved true. In 1963, she fell asleep with the Lord so peacefully and quietly that nobody in the room heard her take her last breath. She was only thirty years old.

That night my father was not at home, nor did he come home until the middle of the night. My mom was very sick, lying on a wooden bed that was built by my grandpa, and the rest of the family slept on the floor on straw mattresses. As my father went to lay down to get some sleep, he asked my mom to move over to make space for him. My little sister was lying by her side from breastfeeding. My mom did not respond.

My father panicked. Everyone was in the same room, so we woke up, startled. I awoke to the devastation and weeping of my family. I walked toward my mom, but my father intercepted me into his arms and held me. My dad quickly removed me from the room. I called for my mother over and over, tears streaming down my face, not knowing what was wrong. I begged my father to let me stay, struggling to free myself from his grasp. He took me to the home of the closest family member, Dragica.

One of the most traumatic moments in my young life was seeing my mom lying in her bed, unresponsive. I was so confused, being so young. Why wasn't she moving? Why was everyone crying? Why wouldn't she answer me? She was dressed in a black blouse with a black scarf, from the death of her mother six months before. (This was a tradition in Serbia. If a family member passed away, we would wear all black all year long and listen to no music.) Men in the household would not shave for forty days in solemn memory of the deceased. She had both hands crossed over her chest. There was a yellow wax candle above her head, lighting the room for family members to mourn around the bed as she laid there peacefully.

I do not remember when I stopped crying, but I remember the next day when my family went to bury my mom. I heard many weeping women outside and ran toward the big window in the house where I was staying. I was able to look from the window out onto the street. One of my family members picked me up and gave me a little pink doll to distract me. The doll was pink plastic, had blue eyes, but no hair or clothes. I was so upset at being removed from the window that I threw the doll at the old wooden door, breaking her. I ran back to the window, only to see the carriage with my mother's coffin being pulled down the road by two cows.

Mourners dressed in black were following behind the carriage as it was pulled up the road. I did not understand much of what was happening at the time except that I couldn't stop crying. I took a deep breath and asked myself, "Was that my mother?" I wanted to be part of the crowd. I wanted to be with her. I ran quickly toward the wooden door. My family member, Dragica, my father's cousin, grabbed me from the door. I tried to wiggle out of her grasp, but she stopped me from leaving the house.

At only three years old, I believe that God allowed me to be mature for a few seconds as I watched out of the window, so I could understand that she would no longer be with us. At the same time, He was protecting me from heartbreak of losing my mother by allowing loved ones to watch after me instead of attending the funeral. This is such a vivid scene for me to remember from so long ago; it is burned in my memory and written in my heart. These are my only memories of my sweet mom.

In those days, there were no telephones to call a doctor or to pass on this information to other family and friends. The deceased remained in the house for one day and night, and then they were buried the next day. The family members would give the deceased their last bath and dress them. There was no pristine morgue or pearl caskets. My mother's wooden coffin and cross were made by neighbors and family who brought their scrap lumber and tools together. In the coffin, a pretty sheet was laid below the body. The wooden top was secured with screws. The family members and friends would dig the grave for the deceased. There was no funeral home or church service. We did not have a church in my village or flowers. I know from attending other traditional funerals that the priest sprinkled holy water and chanted prayers as he swung incense over the grave. In this act of absolution, the priest prayed for the forgiveness of sins, asking God to accept the departed into His kingdom.

Incense symbolized that Christ offered his body and blood. The incense was used as part of the blessings on the deceased and was also viewed symbolically as a farewell as the deceased ascends to God. Friends and family then covered the coffin with dirt and placed little wooden crosses in the ground as a headstone as they mourned. Everyone lit candles, which represented Christ. In His words, "I am the light of the world. Whoever follows me will not walk in darkness, but will have the light of life." A memorial candle lighting was a ceremony with special spoken words about the loved one. We used yellow beeswax candles during these solemn events to represent our grief.

On the day of her burial, my family members prepared traditional food, including my mother's favorite foods, sauerkraut and smoked meat. If we didn't have the money to provide the foods, we borrowed from neighbors. Neighbors in our community borrowed from each other all the time and slowly paid each other back.

We visited her grave one week after the funeral, then forty days later, then six months, and each year afterward by tradition. Unfortunately, her three brothers and one sister never came to visit her resting place or my sister and I. Her other sister, Milka, lived close by and was able to attend the funeral. My uncles and aunt are ashamed of us because we lived in poverty and they have a luxury lifestyle. As I got older, I would visit my mom's resting place two to three times per week, yearning to learn more about her and wanting to see her again. All my mom's family members have passed away.

My mother was very shy, she was the sixth child. My mom had no education and never had a job. She was a good Christian woman. She was always busy working around the house, helping her mom. She helped prepare bed covers with wool thread in beautiful patterns and colors. She also embroidered pillowcases. My mom was very talented with using her hands.

My Dad and I One Year after Moms Death

CHAPTER 3

Life Growing Up

After my mother passed away, Grandma Stana, my father's mother, stepped in to care for me and my little sister. I remember my grandmother so vividly. She had the deepest brown eyes and always wore a scarf on her head. Serbia was governed for hundreds of years by the Turkish law requiring women to wear scarves to cover their heads. She wore a specific sweater without sleeves with six buttons, all different colors and sizes. It was made from itchy wool, the only material she had. You never saw her without an old, faded apron and long skirt, with stockings up to her knees. She would tie the stockings up with a tiny piece of string. She had a wrinkled face and thin gray hair. Grandma Stana was a busy woman, occupied by grandkids or knitting to earn a living. She kept us clothed with her knitting skills and taught me how to knit by age six. She kept us fed, even if it meant she went to bed hungry. She worried over our health, education, safety, and well-being. She prayed over us every night and taught us about God.

My Grandpa Cvetko was a very handsome man. He was tall and thin, with light-blue eyes. I always wished one of his children or grandchildren had inherited his blue eyes, but this did not happen. He wore a traditional dark-green Serbian hat over his bald head. He always wore one pair of pants for weeks on end, patch by patch, until they fell apart. I washed this one pair of pants more times than I could count. I would spend endless hours scrubbing the filth out with a little yellow plastic brush. He had other clothes that were given to him by family members, but he always wore that one pair full of patches, held up around his waist by a thin rope. As he got older, he began losing teeth, which caused him to struggle with chewing corn on the cob, certain fruits, or meats. I was in the fourth grade the first time I watched my grandpa struggle to chew his food. It broke my heart to watch him struggle to eat every day. We didn't have dental insurance to fix this issue. I wanted to help him, but once again, I knew only that God had that power.

Grandpa would ask me to cut his nails when they got too long. Since we did not have clippers, I had to use a knife. He was always worried that I would cut him during his manicure and pedicure since I needed glasses, but of course, we could not afford them. It took me a long time to get this done due to his nails being long and thick. When I was finally done, I would wash his feet and scrub them with a brush. I loved him so much and would do anything for him.

My grandpa never smoked or drank alcohol or did a thing wrong. Grandpa was a hardworking man and quite the woodworker. He longed to make beautiful furniture, but he had a limited number of tools. He made beautiful, strong wagon wheels that had metal banding. He made wooden benches and small chairs for all his grandchildren, so they would have their own little chairs to sit around the wooden table to eat dinner. My grandfather made tall wooden ladders to go up into the attic.

He also made me a beautiful spindle, which I used to collect the thread I made from sheep hair. My grandfather would shear the sheep's wool with scissors. The sheep was happy to get rid of this blanket of wool during the long, hot summers. My grandparents would take the wool to the city to be washed and cleaned. It was bundled up and taken home. My grandma and I used a *kudelja* and *vreteno* that was built by my grandfather. We'd take the strings of wool in our fingers and spin them into yarn. Then we'd take the long strands of yarn and roll them up in a ball. If we wanted colored yarn, we had to buy a color dye. I cherished that spindle, a gift from him. He was always busy at work with building projects. He took great pride in his work.

The village I grew up in Zajmovo only had eighteen homes, each of which would house a family of ten to sixteen people. It's a tradition in Serbia that family members live together under the same roof, because they could not afford to live on their own. Everything anyone owns is passed down through the generations. Only two houses had over ten family members in them. My home had fourteen family members, and my neighbors had seventeen family members living in the same house.

In the village was a small grocery store. A new day began with the rooster's crow and the hungry barking dogs. There was only one business, where an old, frail man worked at putting horseshoes on the horses. You could hear the horses all throughout the village on new shoe days. There was no electricity for an alarm clock or news channel. I never knew the smell of coffee in the air or breakfast like cereal, pancakes, or waffles. I would wake up to the warmth of the straw mat separating me from the dirt of the earth and the wood-burning stove. The kids would fight over who could lay closer to the fire, since it was the only heated room.

Our home and land were located at the bottom of a washed-out slope. It was left to my grandpa after his three half-brothers had the first pick of better land. The land stayed flooded and soggy, just wet enough that crops would not grow. It took weeks of sunshine for his land to dry out. The house was built from old mud bricks, with mud filling in the cracks. It had a little chimney that built up soot every week, needing to be cleaned by me and my siblings.

Like clockwork, we would cut wood every evening to stay warm through the night, then clean up the ashes each morning. Our roof was made of straw until I was about ten years of age, when my father laid very cheap red shingles, which felt like Christmas. Our home had three small windows for the entire house, which allowed us to watch after our animals and protect them from the roaming wolves and coyotes. We would lose our animals occasionally due to the wild wolves in the bitter winters. Losing a chicken, calf, or pig meant much more than it means today. That would put us out of goods such as sugar, flour, or oil for weeks.

There was mud all around the house. We had no fertile grass, no concrete driveway. Fortunately, we did have a fence made of wooden posts and vines from branches. It served many purposes, from keeping our free-range chickens in the yard to hanging clothes out to air dry in the summer air. My father and Grandpa made a little mud scraper to put out by the front door for us to clean our shoes before entering our humble abode.

Grandpa also built an outhouse one hundred yards from our house. During the long, cold winter, the distance seemed even longer. For this reason, during dinner, my grandparents cautioned us against drinking too much. I don't miss those days at all!

Both the exterior and interior of the house were painted white. To make our house look more like a home, we made *zidarice,* pieces of white cloth embroidered with brightly colored thread into pictures, then attached them to the walls of the house with small screws, alongside an icon of Saint Nikola. Since we had no furniture in the house, Grandfather built eleven wooden stools, low to the meal table, and three wooden beds that held three to four kids on each straw-filled mattress. Our one-room house was probably smaller than most living rooms today. There were two smaller outdoor rooms for storage and a small porch with two steps out front.

The house had no carpeting or wood floors…only dirt. The only way to sweep the floor was with a broom we made of wheat straw from the field tied to a wooden pole.

It had to be put into hot water before use so the rope that held it together would stay stronger, lasting longer.

I remember Grandma Stana telling me stories, with her scarred hands crossed over her lap and veins of hard work showing through her frail arms. She shared one particular story on a cold winter's night as the burning wood crackled in the background. The dogs barked outside, protecting us from intruders. I cuddled close to my grandma in an old wooden chair while the oil lamps and glass lanterns provided the lighting. She told me that she once had a younger sister who went to visit her cousin in a faraway village and never returned home. She was very upset to have lost her sister. To this day, she was never found.

I was eleven years old, holding my chin in my little hands, intently listening to her, not knowing that it may be her final years. My curly white hair was tied back with elastic my grandma would use to knit. I wore the knitted wool socks my grandma taught me to make and the leather shoes purchased from the city flea market.

The images of my grandma's stories will stay with me for the rest of my life. She told me my grandfather fought in the Bulgarian-Serbian War. He became a prisoner of war, living in dreadful living conditions and suffering from malnutrition. His life was hanging on by a thread. By God's grace my grandfather and a couple of his friends safely escaped from the prison camp. Unfortunately, thousands of his fellow prisoners died from hunger and diseases. I was disheartened to hear of this and of the brutal Nazi invasion of Yugoslavia and Greece in April of 1941. The Nazis launched a massive air assault on the Yugoslavian capital of Belgrade that killed twelve thousand civilians overnight, the largest number of civilian casualties in a single day of the war. The Nazi soldiers set fire to Serbian villages. She told me of how they shot people execution style in the back of head in front of freshly dug graves or buried them alive. They separated men from women and killed all males between the ages of eight and fifteen years old. Some of the soldiers used bulldozers to drive over the bodies of the dead. They poured gasoline on bodies and burned them in a heap. She told me of how soldiers invaded a gymnasium in Kragujevac killing students, teachers, and professors just to leave them all in a mass grave that only left one survivor to tell the story. This was the saddest day in Serbian history, the country that she loved.

On April 6, 1941, the Serbian military came in the night and woke up my grandfather to go with them to fight the Germans. In Yugoslavia, all men are required to serve in the army for three years without pay. The military would pick up all men from eighteen to sixty years old to transport them to learn how to use weapons and protect the country from invasions of other countries like Germany and Turkey. Serbia lived under Turkish rules for five hundred years. During these times, Turkish forced Orthodox Christians to convert to Muslim. Rejection caused multiple loss of life. Orthodox Christians also converted under pressure from the Turks for safety of the family.

During WWII, German soldiers captured my grandfather and several other young men and took them by train to Germany. They worked as slaves for one long year, building railroads and bridges. They had no communication with their families during this time. My grandma had a difficult time raising her two children by herself, not knowing what had happened to her husband. Fortunately, they were released after rebuilding Germany. One year later, my grandfather's third child was born, Aunt Milanka.

My father was only ten years old when these things happened. Had Russia not intervened and freed us from German and Turkey occupation, my father may not have lived past ten years of age. As soon as my grandparents and other Serbians began to rebuild their lives after the Nazis, Turkish soldiers invaded and destroyed everything they owned. This included killing farm animals, stealing valuables, and forcing the people to change their names and religions. My grandparents, their family, and all other families barely survived this devastating invasion.

Grandma Stana stayed busy with taking care of seven grandchildren. I often wished that my grandparents had a higher income so we could afford nicer things, but she never let any of us go without. I often felt bad that my grandparents had so many responsibilities with grandkids and had no alone time.

Grandma would knit sweaters, socks, scarves, and gloves for each us, because we couldn't afford to buy them. Ladies in the village would gather until midnight around our wooden table with a glowing lantern in the middle to provide light. They would knit kids' clothes while visiting my grandma after putting their children to sleep. They would share thread or wool using different patterns. I would stick next to my grandma like a tick, not leaving her side, even after bedtime.

After learning how to knit and crochet at the age of six, I was hooked. I had a desire to knit all the time. I would sit all day knitting a sweater for the doll I never had. I imagined that one day the sweater I will make will be perfect for my doll. The only problem was, I never had any yarn… But I knew someone who did. Grandma had a green wooden box built by my grandfather, with a lock for her personal belongings. It contained yarn, sugar cubes, coffee, gifts from other family members, and mementos. She kept the key in the pocket of her apron. Sometimes I wanted to knit something, and Grandma had the only yarn, which meant I needed to get that key.

I would hug my grandma and sneak the key out of her apron to raid her yarn stash. I would go through the different colors of yarn and use my teeth to cut two feet of each color. I tied the pieces together and rolled them into a little ball so my grandma wouldn't notice that she was missing yarn of one color. Then I would go back to her, give her a hug, and replace the key without her knowing. I did not want her to find out, so I took great pains to ensure that her box was organized exactly the way I found it. I gathered my yarn and needles, climbed the wooden ladder to the attic, and knitted little clothing accessories for a doll that I never had.

The attic was my hideaway. It was a wooden slab above the whole house where I went to get away and focus. I remember my grandma calling my name, looking for me. I peeped down but did not answer until I used up all the yarn in my secret place. When I finished, I came down to her.

We hardly ever went shopping. When we did, the store was only two minutes down a dusty country road. There was no hot asphalt, honking horns, or bright lights. You would hear singing children, birds chirping, and could see wheat fields for miles. The store was run by a man about my father's age. Metal rods covered the one window protecting the flour, sugar, thread, candy, and oil. The strong wooden door had an iron lock to keep thieves out at night. The store owner would throw out old goods and spoiled food that had expired and he no longer could sale.

During recess at school, all my sisters and the neighbor girls got together and talked of wearing high heels and nail polish. We didn't have such luxuries, but that didn't stop us from dreaming of it. In desperation, we began dumpster-diving behind the store, searching for discarded high heels. I managed to find a pair of burned shoes, which I fished out of the dumpster. I hugged the shoes, praising God the whole way home. When I arrived home, I removed the heels from the shoes. With my grandfather's box of nails, I used a rock as a hammer to nail the heels to the bottom of my flat leather shoes. I stood up in the heels, feeling ten feet tall. I felt so special, beautiful, and rich for a few fleeting moments. Then the pain sunk in, as the nails did in my skin. I had to take the nails out and remove the heels from my shoes. The new holes in my only pair of shoes made them useless at keeping my feet dry on wet days. I've never forgotten the moment when I let my vanity get the best of me.

Besides dumpster-diving for fun, we also liked to play games with the neighborhood kids. One of those games was known in America as jacks. Only we didn't have access to actual jacks, so we used rocks. I believe we made the very first Mr. Potato Head. We would make dolls out of potatoes using sticks for arms and legs and corn silk for hair. I would slice fruit up in thin pieces, stringing them together, making jewelry. We took "playing with food" to a whole new level. We enjoyed "baking" mud cookies as well. We decorated them with grass and sticks. I always decorated mine with little crosses because I loved them. When we would finish, there was a competition as to whose mud cookies were the prettiest. This normally ended in an argument and mud-slinging fight. We also loved playing hide-and-seek, swinging from a plum tree with a chain swing, climbing trees barefooted and riding an old bicycle that had no rubber tires and just a metal seat. We wrapped old towels or pillows on the seat to make it comfortable. We had fun, but all of us had bruises on our legs trying to pedal the bike and keep up with the chain coming off.

My family would grow peppers, cucumbers, potatoes, onions, corn, and wheat during the summertime. Summertime became my favorite season as a child because there was always plenty of produce to eat. During the winter, we struggled. We had to get by on golden cornbread, black bean soup, and boiled potatoes. We had corn on the cob or a baked potato with a little oil and smashed garlic for dinner. If we were lucky, we would add a teaspoon of sugar mixed with water to help the cornbread go down.

We baked our bread outside, on the fire, in a red or black clay pan called *crepulja*. When it rained, we couldn't bake bread, and we had to eat corn on the cob or peel potatoes for dinner. I remember our meals being served on black clay and mud dishes that we would make over the blazing fire.

Our farm was not like a large American farm. It was very small and limited. My family and I only ate meat during the wintertime but we only had the meat when Grandpa would kill an animal and this didn't happen every winter. We had meat for special occasions, and it had to be fresh. In summertime, we did not have a way to prevent the meat from spoiling. When we were sick, Grandma Stana would give us a little meat since the protein would help speed up our healing. Some of the winter, my grandpa provided us with pork butt when snow was on the ground. He buried the meat in the snow and kept it cold so it would stay fresh. Every year, my grandpa would dig a deep hole before the first snowfall. In the hole, he would layer wheat straw, then potatoes covered with more straw, and finally covered everything with dirt. It was called a *trap*. This kept the potatoes from freezing during the long winters and also kept them from rotting.

The produce grew in a field far from our house. We put so much effort into growing vegetables from seed. We grew peppers, cucumbers, tomatoes, green beans, big field of watermelons and cantaloupes. At night, strangers would come to steal them. What they couldn't carry away, they sliced open and left to rot. This happened with our other vegetables as well. We worked so hard to water, rake, and fertilize but had nothing to pick at the end of the season. My grandfather built a little wooden house with a straw roof in the field so he could spend the night, watching over the field with his golden retriever, Zujko, a very protective companion and guard dog.

The intruders found out that my grandfather had a very protective dog and poisoned him. We found him dead in a ditch not far from our home. We were all upset, crying for days. We prayed, then buried him where we found him and visited his grave often. Shortly after, we got another puppy, Zujko, that was raised to be our new protector. To this day, I will never forget him and his friendship.

The only access we had to water was from the well located in front of our house. Birds would occasionally build nests in between the rocks of the well. At times, when I would draw water up, a drowned baby bird would be in my bucket. We used this water for drinking, cooking, bathing, and cleaning. Since we had no washing machine, we had to boil the clothes in the pot on the stove to sanitize them. We also used the water to dilute the milk in a 10 percent to 90 percent ratio to make the milk last longer.

While we were milking a cow on a hot summer morning, flies were in the barn, pestering the cow. She kicked at the buzzing fly, knocking my bucket of milk all over me. My stepmother Stojanka ran out, belittling me for letting the bucket tip over, and she banned me from eating supper with the family as punishment. I was drenched in milk. Since we didn't have showers or running water, I went out to the well to fetch bath water. After heating the water, I went back to the cow barn, where it was somewhat warm and private. Standing on a rock, I scrubbed the milk off me, only to come out smelling like cow manure.

One day after I returned from school, I told my grandma that I was so tired of black beans, cornbread, and soup. Was there anything else she could give me to eat? She pulled me to the side and told me that she had one egg, but I would have to wait until everyone else was asleep. After everyone else was sleeping, I sat beside my grandma, head on her shoulder, and my arms around her neck. She sat in the old wooden chair by the oven, waiting patiently for the egg to cook in the wooden ashes at the bottom of the oven. I was imagining this yummy egg in my stomach and how fast I was going to eat it. Suddenly we heard a loud *bang!* The egg had exploded from the heat and was blasted to smithereens. I was crushed, and my stomach ached from hunger. With tears running down my face, I asked my grandma if there was any leftover black bean soup. I went to bed with no leftovers and no egg. I ended my evening on an empty stomach.

Wintertime was never nice to me. My grandma, at fifty-seven years old, slipped on the icy steps and broke her wrist. The closest doctor was six miles away, but it didn't matter because at that time, we did not have health insurance or money to pay him for services or medication. Fortunately, there was a gentleman known as a healer who never charged the people in his village. He was a very knowledgeable man who knew how to mend broken bones and other ailments. However, he lived ten miles away. My grandpa hurriedly hooked up the wooden wagon to the cows, put my grandma on the straw in the wagon, covered her with blankets, and took off. I still can't imagine how hard it was for her to travel that far with so much pain without medicine, food, or water. It must have taken hours to get there, being pulled by cattle on a cold, slippery road. They left early in the morning and didn't return until dark. I sat inside, praying to God to heal her and return her to me safe and sound. When she returned, the gentleman had fixed her broken wrist by manipulating the bones. He also put her arm in a sling made of a clean cloth. After my grandma left his house, her only hope for healing was to turn to God in prayer. Seeing her in so much pain broke my heart, but she taught me more than I could realize in that moment.

I had to take over many responsibilities when Grandma broke her wrist. I would wash the clothes using her home-made soap made from animal fat and lye. I washed her feet, helped her get dressed, brushed her hair, helped her with her socks, and massaged her legs and back. I always thought that her itchy wool stockings must be uncomfortable, but she never complained. To this day, the images of her in her happiest and saddest moments will never leave my mind. She was the only one person in my young life who taught me about God. I love her much as I love my God, the physician of our soul and body.

Grandkids with Grandpa Cvetko

My Grand Parents in
Every Day Clothes

Relaxing on Grandpa's
Wooden Bench

House Where I Grew Up

Family Old Bicycle

CHAPTER 4

Church and School

We celebrated Christmas on January 7, from the Julian calendar, a day known to Western Christians as Epiphany. However, we start a strict fast from November 28 to January 6. We fast for forty days, which means abstaining from meat, poultry, and dairy products; wine is also restricted. The purpose of fasting is to cleanse the body and the spirit. This was tradition in the old calendar from the Russian Orthodox Church. Before Christmas, we would go into the woods to cut a tiny tree, and we would plant it in an old pot filled with dirt. We then decorated it using handcrafted ornaments. We colored paper and cut out a little star to tie on the top of a tree with a needle and thread. Throughout the year, we would save little pieces of paper and candy wrappers that had been thrown into the street. We put them in between books to flatten them out, then placed little rocks in the wrappers and twisted the ends to make them look like candy. We tied the ends with strands of yarn and hung them on the tree. We also hung family postcards on the tree. My favorite was a postcard with the Nativity scene. Unfortunately, there were no presents to put under the tree. We were not able to go to church very often because of the deep snow. Our Christmases were always white with snow, along with the long, beautiful icicles of different sizes hanging around the house. We would break them off and lick them like ice cream. That couldn't have been healthy, but we never got sick.

The snow was melted by Easter, and we all went to church. We would collect eggs from the chicken coop (an actual Easter egg hunt). They would also be hiding under straw and in bushes. We were allowed to get three eggs each. We colored our eggs with onion skins. This would turn them a yellow-orange color. Another way we colored them was by wrapping leaves around the egg and slipping it into one of Grandma's stockings to hold the leaves and egg in place. This left beautiful patterns on the eggs. I always put crosses on my eggs. While we did not have the money to buy Easter egg dye or new dresses, we did have love for each other, and we thanked God for that. We stuck together and protected one another.

Our village never had a church. With so few people, we had to travel to an Orthodox church seven miles from home. The Christian Orthodox faith has been around for almost twenty centuries. The Orthodox faith is a faith rich in the belief that Jesus is God's only son sent to Earth to live a sinless life only to die for our sins. We pray to icons of Jesus Christ. When entering an Orthodox Church, you smell incense and feel the grace of God. When we make a commitment to live a Christian life, we never cease prayer. Prayer is the key to all things.

Normally, we would walk the seven miles to church. In rainy weather or on special occasions like Easter, we would take the wagon to church. We would fast for forty days. In Serbian and Greek Orthodox religion, fasting meant just water and bread during that time. Everyone except sick people have to fast. When Christians commit to fasting, they give up as well on certain luxuries in order to replicate the sacrifice of Jesus Christ's journey into the desert for forty days, when he was tempted by the devil. Fasting for Easter was not difficult for my family since we fasted the majority of our lives. Most of the time, my grandma wore the same tattered clothes, both at home and church. She didn't have the luxury of a diverse wardrobe like we have today. She took me to church in the same dress that I wore to school and on the farm. I wore the same dress every day to school and was bullied by classmates for that. Grandma always made sure my dress was clean. In the church, all the women covered their heads, wore skirts that covered their knees, and covered their shoulders to show respect to God. This was tradition.

Church gave me an overwhelming feeling that to this day is hard to describe other than to say it was like being wrapped in a hug. The smell of the incense, images of icons, and the sound of praises being sung is still my favorite memory as a child. My grandma would squeeze my hand tightly to make sure I wouldn't get lost in the crowd. There were no chairs, so we would stand in the church for an hour of prayers after traveling so far. In Serbian Orthodox churches, chairs are only located against the wall for the elderly to sit.

Instead of wine as Jesus's blood we received a full table-spoon of honey and an inch square of bread as Jesus's body. I remember asking my grandma if I could take another turn in line to get one more spoonful of the sweet honey and savory bread because it tasted so good. Church was always a special and monumental time in my life. Unfortunately, I didn't have a chance to eat honey again until the next time I went to church.

When I was in third grade, my father and grandparents decided to baptize all six children. The priest came to the house and baptized each of us one at a time. It was not a big formal ceremony, but it signified our new life in Christ.

There was no celebrating birthdays or anniversaries in my family due to the lack of money. We never bought, made, or swapped gifts. We never sang to each other. I can recall one occasion my father got me a bag of candy. It was such an exciting time. I carried it to school and shared it with twenty classmates. It felt so special to share this joy with others. However, I did not have a piece of candy left-over for me, just an empty bag.

School began when I turned seven. The children in the village would all walk the two and a half miles together. Many times, we were attacked by kids of other religions who stood on the side of the road with handfuls of rocks. As we drew near, they would pelt us with rocks and tell us that one day we would have to leave our country. I was hit in the head with a rock thrown by a little girl who was about seven years old who I didn't even know. When I asked her why she did it, she replied she didn't like Christians. I still have a mark on my head from that rock. We had no place to go and report these incidents. If we complained, the situation would only get worse and expose ourselves to more danger. We received many threats, telling us if we didn't move, they would hurt us. We had dogs outside to warn us of approaching strangers.

I only had one pair of shoes, and as my feet grew, those shoes got too small. To give my feet growing room, I cut the top of my shoes off (in what would look like sandals today) so that my toes would no longer hurt and to make room for my toes to grow. Since I wore these shoes for such a long time, they wore thin. I began getting holes from rocks in the bottom of the soles. My feet would often get wet on rainy days and freeze when it snowed. I wore the same clothes every day, and the other kids avoided me like the plague. I was bullied in school for my poverty, my hair, my yellow teeth (no toothbrush, paste, or regular dental check-ups), and my poor eyesight or not having glasses to see the chalkboard. I was never invited to their birthday parties.

I would leave home every morning at 7:00 a.m. to be on time for class at eight o'clock. My grandma would hug me goodbye, sad that she didn't have breakfast to give me. Even without food, I was still excited about going to school. The school wouldn't provide breakfast or lunch, so we would go without food during the day. My stomach would send roaring growls throughout class until I could get home at 3:00 p.m. It was hard to stay focused and study when the pit in my stomach would hurt so badly and my brain only thought of food.

My school had two classrooms on a little hall with blue-framed glass windows, a blue door, and a red shingled roof.

The exterior was unpainted cement. The two classrooms were divided by Serbian and Albanian students from first to fourth grade. Each classroom had small wooden desks with small shelves underneath for books and supplies with little wooden seats. The classrooms had a green chalkboard and a bare lightbulb that hung from the ceiling.

First grade through third grade, I had my first teacher, Dragich Bogavac. He was a little man with light brown hair with eyebrows and eyelashes that were almost white. He always wore a suit and tie with nice shoes to go with them. He would rub the top of my head and tell me to keep up the good work. He noticed that I had a desire to learn, so he gave me extra attention. I became an A student and never received punishment from him (which was allowed if warranted).

However, my fourth-grade teacher, Milena Krasich, gave me my first school spanking. She hit me on my hands with a twig for not doing my homework. We had to hold our hands out with palms facing up and received five or six lashings. If you moved your hands, you received double. The whippings left red welts that stung to the touch. She did them out of love, only wanting to discipline her students. After this punishment, we all became better students.

My teacher was beautiful, tall, and blond with blue eyes. She always wore lovely dresses with high-heel shoes. I loved to look at her high heels and thought to myself that one day I will have those type of shoes. She rode a bicycle to work every day and was a dedicated educator. I soon realized that this grade was a lot harder. I had no one at home to help with my studies.

The maintenance man named Martin who worked in our school would bring the children water in a tiny pitcher. The kids would pass around a little metal blue cup with a handle and share the water from it. He also brought in firewood to heat our classrooms. There was no indoor plumbing, but there was a very long walk to an outhouse. When it rained and during the winter, the walk felt much longer. Every day was the same situation. We struggled to survive, read our Bibles, and prayed for our God to save us.

In the fifth grade, I had to change schools. I was required to take courses in Russian and Albanian languages. The Russian instructor, Milutin Brcanovich, required us to greet him in Russian every time he walked in and out of the classroom. He was tall and skinny with a bald head and big ears. My Albanian professor was just the opposite. He was short with lots of brown hair. He was also extremely strict. If our homework was not completed, students would be failed at the end of the school year and have to take the class again.

No matter how my day had been, I hummed and sang constantly. My angelic voice caused classmates, neighbors, friends, and professors to plead with me to sing for them. My biology professor once had a heartbreak from a young woman leaving him, so he begged me to sing sad songs in the middle of class, in front of everyone. He expressed that the songs made him feel better. He always wore a silver suit, slick black shoes, and long hair reminding me of Jesus.

My friends from school constantly talked about their moms—moms who would brush their hair, make them a warm breakfast, or help them with their homework. I did not have any of these experiences or stories. I finally realized that my mom would not be coming back to me, but I never stopped visiting her grave. Many times after school, I would visit my mom's grave. It wasn't very far from school. It was easier to visit in the summer than in the winter, but I loyally visited her, even in the winter. My hands would turn blue from the cold, and the bangs of my hair would freeze. My wool gloves and scarf wouldn't provide much heat.

I knelt by her grave and spoke to her every chance I got. I would tell her absolutely everything, from my ordinary day at school to the things that hurt me deeply. I covered my face with my hands and would cry and cry and cry frozen tears. When I would yell for her, I would cup my hands over my mouth to deepen my voice hoping she'd hear me. I thought if I cried loud enough, my mom would hear me and come home. I wiped the tears with the sleeves of my shirt. Every time I visited her grave, I felt that God was watching over me. Anything could've happened to me. I was fearless in the pursuit to visit my mother's grave. Someone could have snatched me, and there were wild animals all around. I went anyways. After every visit, I left disappointed and sad. I put my sadness into God's hands and thanked him for my grandma because I knew that my mom was watching over us.

By the time that school had ended and I finished visiting my mother, I ran to embrace my grandma. I was so skinny, and the kids at school made fun of me. None of my other family members were educated, so they couldn't help me with my homework, nor did they show any interest in my studies. There was no table or desk for me to do my work on. I didn't have any papers or books to use while studying. Lastly, the constant presence of so many people in one room was so distracting that studying was made difficult. I sat on the dirt floor with my homework in my lap and studied alone anyways. I was the only child of my father's nine children to complete all twelve grades.

On the way home from school, the kids would pass a *trnjine* bush. Trnjine are similar to blueberries. The kids would hang on it and climb around like goats to snack on the juicy fruit. We would fill our little bellies with dusty trnjine, wondering if there was going to be anything to eat at home or if we would have to go to sleep without dinner. Before we went home, we would be scratched and bleeding from the trnjine's thorny bushes.

Behind our house were about twenty plum trees, which we used to make a drink called *sljivovica*. This was an alcoholic beverage that served many purposes. It was an all-around health tonic. Our parents would rub it on the bottoms of our feet and chests whenever the kids had a fever or cold. Usually, the men drank tiny shots in the morning for their cholesterol. The plums were collected in big barrels and fermented. The liquid was drained through heated pipes, then poured into glass bottles. The slivovica would last ten years or even more. The longer it sat, the better it got. The leftover plum skins would then go to the compost heap. Plum trees helped us to survive. Sometimes we couldn't wait for the plums to ripen and would eat them while they are still green. The green plums were sour and gave us stomach aches, but at times, we didn't have anything else to eat.

When I was eight years old, I was walking behind my house and noticed that all the plums had fallen to the ground. Nothing was worth eating. I spotted the juiciest, ripest plum about twenty-five feet up the tree. I was so hungry, and the plum was calling my name. I was determined to get that plum. I climbed like a monkey with my bare feet up the tree. I was a mere five inches away from my goal, when the plum fell to the ground and burst. I was absolutely crushed… Just like the plum.

We had a three-month summer break from school, which we spent working on the farm. I would get together with the neighbor kids. We would move the livestock to the fields so they could graze. We also would build a fire to bake corn on the cob for our daily meal. We ate so much corn that when it came time for my father to harvest it, there was not much left on the stalks. He was not happy with us. We did the same thing with the potatoes. We had to eat something. During the summertime, my neighbor kids and I packed our family's dirty clothes into burlap bags and carried them on our backs for three miles to the Beli Drim River. We took a pot with handles, laundry soap, and we used water from the river. We dug a hole with our bare hands into the damp earth and built a blazing fire to put the pot of water over to boil and kill bacteria when washing our clothes. We rinsed the clothes in the river, wrung them out, and threw them on top of nearby bushes to dry. While they were drying, my friends and I frolicked in the river, splashing and jumping around. We bathed with the same soap that we washed clothes with when we were done playing. We had the happiest times in our lives down by that river, which is now dried up. When the clothes dried, we folded them neatly, making sure to do such a good job that we would not have to iron them, put them in the burlap bag, and carried them along with the pot back home.

After eighth grade in my country, you have to decide your career path. We began learning how to work in different areas. I chose to be a cashier and went three times a week to practice operating a cash register. My favorite place to practice was a two-story mall close to my school. We did not get paid for this, although at the end of the shift, if the register had an extra dollar or two, the instructor let me have the money, which I used for a piece of bread and hazelnut spread, a big reward for me.

My School from First to Fourth Grade

CHAPTER 5

Krsna Slava

In the Serbian Orthodox practice known as Krsna Slava, every Orthodox family in Serbia has one patron saint. The saint is celebrated by a yearly feast on the Julian calendar, December 19. Every family has a different saint, but Saint Nikola is the most common patron saint for Serbian families. Saint Nikola was a Christian bishop who was known for providing for the poor and sick. He constantly prayed for them and shared everything that he owned. He lost both of his parents as a young man and used his inheritance to help others. We believe this saint is one of the biggest protectors of Christian people, sailors, and marines, and he remains the family's patron saint from generation to generation, passed down by father to his son like a torch. Serbian people believe he protects their homes and belongings. Saint Nikola's feast day falls during the Advent fast or Nativity fast on November 15 and lasts for forty days in preparation for the Nativity of Jesus on December 25. While the feast has a tradition of celebrating with rich foods, meat and dairy products are not allowed on that day. However, fish is allowed to eat on the fast day. Even when my family did not have the money to celebrate this saint's day, my father borrowed money so that we would have fish for the special occasion. My family, along with others, show respect and love for Saint Nikola by keeping his icon on their walls.

December is the best time to celebrate indoors for parishioners because of the cold temperatures, hard grounds, and snow. Plenty of time to be with family for praying, singing, and dancing. The most important part of this occasion I experienced was when my grandpa took me with him to church for Krsna Slava ceremony. The lady of the house makes a traditional decorated, baked bread. Then the owner of the house delivers a bottle of red wine and the bread to the church which has a cross centered on the top crust. Bread is cut by the priest as he makes the sign of the cross. He turns the Slavski bread over, slices a cross symbol on the bottom of the bread, and pours red wine through the opening as a symbol that Christ died on the cross and shed blood for the remission of our sins. The priest performs a special prayer for the health of the families, prosperity for the year, and protection from evil. After liturgy, family members take wine and bread home to share with all other family members and guests. The male head of the house can also perform this special ceremony at home, which was my grandpa. Slava is a family reunion usually held in the home of the family's oldest living member to commemorate the patron saint and glorify God. Friends and neighbors need no invitation or reservation; they simply need to show up. This event is a time for spiritual renewal and rededication to the Orthodox faith and church.

Four elements must be present on the table in an Orthodox home. The first is the Slavski bread, Kolac, as Jesus Christ is the bread of life. Then bread is distributed to the family members, with some saved for the first guest to enter the house. The second is a lit beeswax candle which represents the light of Christ. Christ is the light of the world. Without light, we would live in darkness. The third item is red wine, which represents Christ's precious blood that washes away our sins. The fourth item is slavsko zhito, which is cooked wheat placed on a plate and decorated with a cross from shelled almonds or walnuts, which symbolizes the resurrection and eternal life. It is prepared for the glory and honor of the family's patron saint.

During one particular Slava celebration, my stepmother's youngest brother was one of our guests. This young man refused to respect the fasting rules and eat the fish or any of the other prepared traditional food and demanded that my grandfather climb into the attic and bring down some of the smoked pork he kept stored. My grandfather, wanting to remain observant of the church's fasting rules, did not want to do this. My stepmother's brother kept pressuring him. My grandfather was so frustrated with his behavior and gave in. He climbed the ladder to the attic, grabbed a piece of the meat, and climbed back down the wooden ladder. As he descended, he fell and broke his leg. My father loaded him up in the wooden wagon pulled by cows and took him to the same man who fixed my grandma's wrist. He confirmed that grandpa's leg was broken, splinted it, and sent him home. My stepmother's brother enjoyed the pork while grandpa was in agony. Grandpa regretted breaking fasting rules and we all thought this accident was a curse from God. After this accident, we never violated the fasting rules again.

Arrangement for Krsna Slava of St Nikola

CHAPTER 6

Lola, Stanica Knezevich, and Stojanka

My maternal grandfather, Milan, played Cupid with my father's third wife, Lola. She lived across the road from him and had grown up knowing my mom. Father married her one year after Mother passed away. They soon had a little girl named Bozana. When Lola would go see her family, we would go with her and get to visit our grandfather. Since he was financially broke and could not afford train tickets, he rarely came to see us. What might seem odd for a man to find his previous son-in-law a wife was just Grandpa showing pure love. My grandpa knew that Father needed a woman.

Lola was tall and beautiful. She reminded me of my mom at instances. They both wore their hair in a long braid covered with a traditional scarf. One difference was that her left leg was shorter than her right leg.

She was in very poor health. I remember that she would have stomach issues whenever she ate. She could not eat cornbread and suffered. She also did not like living in a house shared by multiple family members. This caused a lot of problems within their marriage. She soon left my father and took my half-sister with her to live with her parents in the mountains of Krtok. She couldn't handle a life with few food choices and in-laws who bossed her around (especially my uncle).

After she left, we have no chance to see our sister. Since my father was jobless, he had no money to support my half-sister. He received so many angry letters from Lola for not sending money to support their child. After that, she refused to allow my half-sister to have any contact with us.

When I was fifty-five years old, I went to Serbia to visit my family. I was able to see my half-sister for the first time after fifty years. I discovered that she looks the most like my father out of all my siblings. We spent time together, but we felt like strangers because of the time spent apart. I found that she has a kind, generous personality, and we decided to stay in touch to make up for lost time.

After Lola never came back, Stanica came into the picture less than a year later. I was five years old at the time and living with my grandparents, so I do not remember much about her. Stanica was never married and had no children. She was only with my father for a short period of time. My father neglected to mention that he was married three times previously and had four children. When one of her brothers found out, her brothers began to threaten my father. They wanted to hurt my father. He did not think that his life and the life of his children should be put at risk. My father's good sense kicked in, and he let her go.

He finally found his woman, who was fifteen years younger than him. I remember when my new stepmother, Stojanka, came into my life. She had short, curly, brown hair and light-colored freckled skin. Her teeth were very spread out, and she was smaller than his previous wives. One year later, my dad and Stojanka had a son, Milosav. As a little girl, I was jealous of the attention that my father gave to my stepmom.

Stojanka grew up in the mountains (like three of his previous wives—anytime my father needed a new wife, he would find them in the mountains), isolated from the city, and she had no connection with any neighbors or men in general. Her family rode a donkey down to the city once a month to shop for oil, sugar, flour, and gas for lanterns. It was their only opportunity to talk with other people. She came from a family of six children. She had never been married or had any experience with children. Growing up so isolated and having no experience with kids made her very selfish. She had to adjust her lifestyle to raising three stepdaughters. Her being so immature, she was mean, bossy, and abusive. She told us that we were ugly, that no one would marry us, and that she hoped we would never be happy. She went to the neighbors and bad-mouthed us, saying terrible things. She never had a kind word for us and showed no affection. If you didn't obey her rules, you were yelled at or spanked, then given the silent treatment. I forgive her, as God wants me to. She refused to allow us to keep any clothing items, bedspreads, or linen that belonged to our mother. At the time, I couldn't understand why she acted the way she did, but now as a grown woman, I hold nothing against her. My stepmom was married at such a young age, with so many new responsibilities. Now understanding what she was going through, I don't completely blame her. My father was very happy to have her in his family. He thought he'd finally found the love of his life.

I will never forget the time when I was not feeling well. I never had energy, but I would carry six liters of milk four miles to the city of Klina and sell in the mornings. All the money collected was given to my stepmom, and I never received any allowance for my work. This made me sad because I could not buy anything to eat. I was not a perfect kid at all times because my stepmom had so many rules. On this particular day when I was ill, I had enough of her rules. I didn't want to get up to do my chores. She ran in, chased me, and went to hit me, so I jumped out of a window. I landed on top of broken glass bottles that were on the ground under the window. I cut my leg and was bleeding profusely. I needed stitches, but I didn't have a way to get them. I simply washed the wound and wrapped an old shirt around it until it healed. The scar is still there today, but so am I, thanks to God.

When I was six, Stojanka attempted to give me a bath in a small metal tub in front of the woodstove, so that I would be warm. My stepmom was in such a hurry to bathe me, and she was rushing me, causing me to slip and hit my face on the side of the hot stove. My skin was stuck like glue to the side of the stove. It was agonizing. Stojanka never apologized or wiped my tears away. She just walked away. Fortunately, my grandparents were there to help me. Nobody took me to the doctor to take care of my burns, but they used natural healing leaves, *bokvica*, mixed with cow manure and ink. They placed the combination on my wounds. That healed my burns but left a scar. Bokvica was also used to clear up boils on the skin.

My stepmother's cooking wasn't much to brag about. She used copious amounts of salt on everything, so much that my tongue would hurt and I couldn't swallow the food. She made bread to last the entire week, which ended up getting hard and stale. It got moldy quickly during the summer, but we couldn't afford to let it go to waste.

My stepmother baked chicken and bread on days my father worked in the fields so that he would have plenty of energy. The cows pulled the plow with my father behind them while I dropped the corn and bean seeds in the hole. My father planted the wheat, holding the bag of seeds in one hand and spreading them with the other. After the wheat is harvested, it is taken to a mill to have it grinded into wheat flower. The wheat was needed to make bread.

Everything came back to life in the spring. Leaves sprouted on trees, the birds returned to sing, and the children came back outside to play. Spring also brought with it the arrival of new baby animals. We loved playing with the little piglets, calves, chicks, ducks, geese, puppies, and kittens. I remember always being followed by baby ducks around the outside of house as I fed the chickens and did my chores.

The rooster is considered the protector and king of his pen. When we bent down in the pen, the rooster would jump on our backs. My father and grandfather built a chicken coop with a wooden ramp and door for the chickens to stay in at night. My siblings and I took turns making sure the door was locked each night to keep the foxes, raccoons, and opossums out of the chicken coop.

My father liked having me work with him in the fields since I was always so eager to help him. We left in the morning at four, before the sun came up, and we would come home around 11:00 a.m. because of the extreme heat. We walked for an hour, carrying our rake, sickle, and pitchfork with us on our shoulders. We had nothing to eat for breakfast or take with us and no water either. We worked together in the cornfield, pulling weeds. We would also work in the pasture, using a pitchfork to dry the hay for the animals. Once the sun rose, shortly after 7:00 a.m., the heat and hard work started making me sick. Once we finished our work and began the long walk home, I would start to lose steam. I would sit down and rest while my father went ahead of me. I didn't want to complain to my father too much.

I didn't realize at the time that I was hypoglycemic. This means that my blood sugar level was below normal range. I was completely out of energy, after eating very little and working very hard. Shaking and sweating, I would lie down and fall asleep. Anything could have happened during the times I passed out. I could have been bitten by a snake or attacked by an animal. But during that time and many other times, nobody but God still sustained me, and I know I was never alone. I strongly believe that God fed me through the air and woke me up with energy to carry me home. This incident happened several times. Since we did not have air-conditioning, we put blankets over the windows to keep the hot summer heat out. This also helped keep the flies out. You couldn't sleep when swatting flies.

Between my mom and three other stepmoms, my father had ten children; nine lived and one was deceased. His life was very complicated. He and my stepmother argued about everything. They did not have jobs, but they kept having kids without any means to support them.

Stojanka delivered my half-brother, Milosav, on a train. Her midwife and brother-in-law were with her, headed to the hospital. Since it was a train, there were no supplies. My uncle used his own jacket to wrap the baby up. My uncle did not report this event to the train conductor. If he had, Milosav could have had a job at the train station and lifetime free travel to any destination, the midwife who delivered the baby and my stepmom told us this story, but my uncle was afraid if he reported it, he would be required to pay to clean up the train car. It was a miracle to have a baby on a train without any medical supplies, diapers, or painkillers for my stepmom.

All my half-brothers and sisters, including myself, were born well before disposable diapers. We would use cloth diapers made from old shirts and rope. Babies didn't wear clothes for three months. My grandpa made a wooden, rocking cradle that you could sit next to and rock with your foot. The pillow was made from wheat straw. Warm wax was put in the umbilical cord of newborns for about a week until it fell off. Mothers prayed to be able to breastfeed their babies. Baby bottles were not available, nor could we afford formula. If there was not enough milk, we would dilute it with water. This was very difficult during the winter, when there was no milk because the cows were nursing their calves. We had no cameras, nor did we have money to pay somebody to take baby pictures. Most of all my brothers and sisters were born at home. My dad was not able to participate in the birth of his children. Unlike today, the father was not allowed in the delivery room. My father happened to be working away from home. He was delighted to hear about the birth of his son Milosav after having three girls. Bozana was the fifth child out of ten, so there were four girls (with her, Vera, me, and Grozda). One year later, Momirka was born. Stamena was born two years later, then Jelena two years later. My father started multiplying like a rabbit. Dragan was the only other boy and born last. Every two years brought a new baby and an expansion to our family.

CHAPTER 7

Grandma's Death

When I was just twelve years of age, I had a nightmare of walking barefoot down a country road to visit my friends. In the middle of the road, a snake came out of the bushes and bit me on the bottom of my left foot. It was so terrifying and painful that upon waking up, I checked to see if I'd actually been bitten. My grandfather woke up and when he asked me what was wrong, I told him about my nightmare. He told me that in his experience, nightmares like this meant that someone was about to pass away.

Grandma was sixty years old when she got very sick. She had some type of lung infection. Her fever would spike higher than we could cool her down. My stepmom and aunt tried using natural remedies. They tried using *aksencija*, a liquid stronger than vinegar, to help bring down her high fever. They soaked a towel in it and would put it on her chest. It ended up only giving her large, shiny blisters on her skin. The last thing I remembered her doing was calling for water over and over. She was so thirsty but too weak to drink it. As Grandpa held her tightly in his arms, she passed away on his warm, beating chest. Losing my grandma, I was heartbroken. I'm going to miss her hugs, stories, prayers. She was my guardian angel.

My grandma was put in a wooden coffin built by neighbors and friends, then buried next to my mom. Grandma was buried with a gift given to her by my mother. It was a beautiful ćilim, a colorful, patterned blanket made of wool. We placed it underneath her. When I would visit my mom's resting place, I'd sit between their graves, crying and talking for hours with both of them, the women who shaped me.

My grandma's passing was one of the hardest things in my life since the death of my mother. I began to become fearful of who would take care of me, take me to church, or pray with me. I adored my grandmother and learned so much from her. She taught me about God, Communion, and how to be a good person. I worried about my future without her. I still had my grandpa and father left. My father continued diligently chasing women to find the love of his life, so he wasn't always around. The same goes for my grandpa. After her death, Grandpa became deeply depressed and ran away from home. He stayed gone for two days until we found him in the woods, weeping. Grandpa encouraged me to stay close to God and told me that one day, I would be able to move on with my life.

With my grandmother now gone, it was my job to do the family's laundry. Life had to go on, so I had to take on more responsibilities. I would pull water from the well, the weight of which would sometimes break the rotten, weak rope that held the bucket. My father had to go down eight to ten meters deep to get the buckets. I put the water on a pot on the oven and boiled the clothes to kill the bacteria. I would then hang the clothes out to dry. So many times, a rainstorm would come through, and I would have to rewash the clothes. In the wintertime, we would hang the clothes to dry on a clothesline above the woodstove.

Shortly after my grandma's passing, my father was able to install electricity in our house. We had a little, old, black-and-white TV with only two channels. Of course, we were too busy working on our farm to watch TV. At sunset, when all the chores were done, the neighborhood kids would come to our house to watch TV with us. Everyone found a space on the floor, but I would stand next to the TV because of my bad vision.

CHAPTER 8

Off to Work

When I was thirteen, my father went to work in Germany. He was raising white mice for lab testing for disease research. My father returned home one year later and brought back many different sizes of used clothing from his boss's wife. He arrived late at night, so we didn't see him until the next morning. My stepmother picked through everything, choosing what she wanted while we slept. Out of the things that were left, nothing fit us. My sister Grozda took one extra-large sweater, which she tried to alter herself.

As Grozda tried sewing the sweater, the room was very dark. She put the light on to see, and my stepmom demanded she turn it off. My sister refused, so my step-mother turned the light out. My sister complained that she needed the light to see and turned it back on. My step-mother slapped my sister like a mule several times in the head. I cried with my sister, and we sat in the dark, afraid to turn the lights back on. At that time, my sister believed that my stepmom was her birth mother. I explained that our real mother passed away.

My father continued to work in Germany for two years and sent money home to the family. My uncle would always take the money, deciding how it would be spent.

We discovered that my grandfather had cancer. We sent a letter to my father to tell him that his father was very ill. My dad quit his job in Germany to come back home because he knew that my uncle would not do anything to help my grandfather. He suffered in pain for a long time. All of us being in the same room had to endure the sleepless nights with him, as he screamed in excruciating pain. The cancer spread through his throat, creating a hole in his neck so that he couldn't eat or drink. He passed away at the age of seventy-two and was buried on the other side of my mom's grave. Three days before his passing, my father called the priest to say prayers for him. My grandparents wished to be buried around my mom, because they had so much love for her. He was placed in a wooden coffin built by neighbors and family members who also built my mom's and grandma's. We held the same traditional ceremony as before for my mom and grandma. These were three dear lives snatched from mine before I even reached high school.

After my grandfather passed, things in my life became much more difficult. My younger sister, Grozda, was ten, and taking care of Stamena, Jelena, and Dragan. She fed, bathed, and dressed them and comforted them when they cried. She always carried the youngest one on her back. When she went to draw water from the well, she tied the baby on her back with a rope behind the knees so that he wouldn't fall in as she leaned over the well. She was never able to finish her schooling, because she was always caring for my stepmother's kids.

I remember washing a mountain of clothes that Stojanka brought to me on the open porch in the crisp winter air. She had me rinse the clothes outside at the well as my fingers turned blue and lost their feelings. My ears and eyelashes would freeze and feel hard to the touch, like stone, as snow mounded on my shoulders.

Grozda and I never had secrets between us. We always looked out for each other, encouraged each other, and prayed together. She was my best friend. My sister looked a lot like my mother. She loved to take care of kids. She did not like to brush her hair. She was the favorite girl to my stepmom, Stojanka. She did not finish high school after tenth grade because she could not afford it and had no school supplies. She would hide in the bushes around the school instead of going into class until the teacher noticed it and contacted my father. When school finished, she would walk home with the rest of the kids.

My Sister Grozda and Me

CHAPTER 9

Teenage Dreams

When I was around sixteen, roads were built through our village. We got public buses for transportation. The buses would pass back and forth, three times a day. My neighborhood classmates and I wanted to find a faster way home from school. We were supposed to purchase tickets from the driver at the front of the bus, but since we had no money, many times we would sneak in through the back door and pray to God that we don't get caught. When the inspector went through the bus checking for tickets. He found that none of us had tickets and was reported to the bus driver who kicked us off the bus. We are thankful he wouldn't take us to the police, but we would have to walk the rest of the way home in the blazing heat.

There were no bus shelters, just a tiny wooden sign that said "Bus." The buses had wooden seats and metal poles, and they were always full of standing people. With so many people, plus their bags full of goods to sell at the market, it was always a tight squeeze. Naturally, this lack of space led to arguments about who would get a seat. One day, I was standing in a bus with my friends, surrounded by many foreign young men. The men would hold onto our hips and try to grope us. We tried to move, but they wouldn't let go. I wanted to do something. The men threatened us by flashing a glance at their pocketknives. They would tell us that if we moved, we would pay for it. We felt so embarrassed and violated. I got off the bus as soon as I could. Just like the kids with the rocks at the roadside, there was no one we could tell and nothing we could do. Many parents waited for their children at the bus station every night to make sure they got off the bus safe. There were bad incidents and missing girls in the area where we lived, and our parents didn't want the same thing to befall us. My father and other parents took turns meeting us at the bus station because he didn't want the same thing to happen to us that happened to his aunt when she disappeared while traveling to visit her cousin.

My father was very strict, so he refused to let us date or have boyfriends without supervision. There were handsome young men in our village, but our father was so afraid that someone would hurt us or we would get pregnant and bring shame to our family. A young, unmarried, pregnant woman would be abandoned by her family and left to raise her children alone. Most of the time, she would be unable to find a man who would marry her. As a socialist country, there was no government assistance, health insurance, or food stamps. In an effort to further curtail any potential pregnancy risks, our father tried to dissuade us from using makeup, nail polish, or from plucking our eyebrows. Instead, he wanted us to keep our big bushy eyebrows like a cat's tail. He reminded us that God made us so pretty, we didn't need all of those beauty products.

I remember when visiting a friend, Zorica, in the village, she offered me some of her orange nail polish. I loved it, more than what I worried about what my father might say. When I got home, I tried to avoid having my father notice my hands during dinner. I distinctively remember holding my spoon like a caveman so that my nails weren't noticeable. He knew something was up and demanded to see my hands. He ordered me to leave the table and remove the offensive nail polish. Not having nail polish remover, I had to scrape it off with a knife or a piece of broken glass. It took an hour and that was so painful, lesson learned. I didn't touch nail polish for years.

My father would not let his sister, Milanka, leave the house without a head covering. When she did not have a scarf, she had to put a shirt on her head by Turkish law. That made my aunt so angry.

When it came to haircuts, we put a pot around our siblings' heads and used a pair of sheep shears to trim their hair. This had to be the origin of the bowl cut. We took a bath once a week and shared a hairbrush with everyone in the family. I had long, thick, curly blonde hair that was difficult to tie back, so my grandma had always given me the elastic from her stockings to use as ponytail holders.

When I turned seventeen, many neighbors started to sell their homes and move away from our village. Pressure from other countries began to rise as foreign families began moving into our village. Men would buy wives and overpopulate our community, bringing three wives and twenty children into one home.

I graduated from high school in 1978. Even though I had the desire to go further, I had no money and no scholarship. Since the government controlled everything, teenagers struggle to find jobs after graduation in Serbia. People would only give their family members jobs. The only other ways to get a job were to pay someone off or leave the country.

My father had to find seasonal work in construction jobs, which didn't pay very well. My father began looking for work in a place that was safer, more secure, and promised a better future. One day, he told us of the new job he had accepted. This new job would give him the supplies he needed to build a small starter home.

It was during this time that I left home at the age of nineteen. I saved enough money to buy a train ticket by selling leftover white beans from the fields in the market. I struck out for Belgrade, the capital of Serbia, to a village sixteen miles away called Simanovci to visit my half-sister Vera. She lived in a one-room apartment with her husband and four kids. I began to look for employment anywhere that would hire me. During the first week of staying with my half-sister, I found a job working in a place that made wooden embroidery hoops (wood frames for needlepoint pictures). I was very happy to be hired and to have an actual paying job for the first time in my life. I didn't even ask what the pay was. I was just proud to be working.

After I moved to Belgrade, I received several letters from Grozda about how much work she had picked up since I left home. Because she was so busy taking care of our younger siblings, she had to stop going to school. Six months after I started working, I asked the owner if he would hire my younger sister, and he agreed. With the little money I'd saved, I bought a train ticket to return to Kosovo and bring my sister back to Belgrade with me. When I returned to Kosovo, I didn't tell anyone, even her, that the reason I'd returned was to bring Grozda to Belgrade with me. I saw my sister washing clothes on the porch in front of our house. She was surprised and very excited to see me. We hugged each other for a minute and shared joyful tears.

I told her that I was taking her with me, but what I didn't realize was that my stepmother was eavesdropping on our conversation. Suddenly, my sister yelled, "Watch out!" As I turned around, there stood my stepmother with a shovel in her hand. She cursed and spat on me. I grabbed the shovel from her hands before she could hit me in the head with it. She was unhappy that I had left and now I was taking my sister with me. Without us there to do the chores, that meant more work for her. We packed my sister's clothes in a few plastic bags and left that same day. As we left the house, my stepmother was still holding that shovel behind me and saying horrible things. As we ran off, she shouted, wishing we would get sick, never heal, be alone forever, and never find happiness. There were no kind hugs or goodbye words exchanged.

Grozda was so happy to be leaving but also scared. My sister and I walked six miles to the train station during the night. We sat on the wooden benches, thinking about our stepmother's wrath and worrying that my father would come looking for us. We prayed that for once, the train would be on time. We waited for two hours, praying that my father would not show up to take us home. Our anxiety reached another level as the train was delayed. I hung on to the scripture in Isaiah 41:10 that says, "Do not fear, for I am with you." My sister was pale and shaking from the fear that our father would show up and from lack of food.

The train finally arrived at 10:30 p.m., and along with it, our freedom. We sat in the wooden seats of the coal-powered train, looking out the dirty windows with the grungy brown and green curtains. Our stomachs were empty, but our hearts were celebrating and thanking God for protecting us. Exhausted after all the drama with my stepmother and the anxiety we felt at the train station, we fell asleep sitting up in the wooden seats, interrupted only by the train conductor asking for our tickets.

Eight hours later, we were in Belgrade. We arrived at the city around 7:30 a.m. It was glittering with lights. We walked through the city, carrying my sister's clothing in plastic bags, among the elegantly dressed crowds in the street. Street vendors were setting up their magazine stands and little sidewalk cafés. My sister and I had enough change between us to buy two pastries. Our hair was dirty and bushy, and our clothes were wrinkled. As we walked toward the bus station, we joked about how awful we looked. But we knew that we were now free, thanks to our Heavenly Father. We didn't have to listen to our stepmom, and we were able to change our life for the better. We purchased our bus tickets to travel the sixteen miles from Belgrade to Vera's apartment. On the ride there, my younger sister was astonished by how beautiful and green the countryside was. When we arrived, Vera welcomed us with soup, Polish kielbasa, and bread. Then she allowed us to freshen up we all sat on the old brown couch and talked about our trip and the drama with our stepmom when we left the house for the last time.

When we awoke, I took my sister on a tour of the village to show her where she would be working, along with the grocery store, bakery, hair salon, and restaurant. When we returned from our walk, we thanked Vera for her generosity and asked her for help in finding a place to live. She had her husband and four children to care for, and we didn't want to impose any longer than necessary. That night, we slept on a small, thin mattress and left the next morning for work. We stopped on the way at the store for half a loaf of bread and some chicken spread called *pasteta* for our breakfast and lunch.

We arrived at work, and I introduced my sister to my boss. There were no employment documents to sign and no benefits. She knew that we would get paid, but she didn't know how much. After our shift ended that day, my sister and I began apartment hunting. We didn't have classified ads. We simply walked from house to house, asking if the owners had an extra room they would be willing to rent to us.

We finally came to a house where a seventy-year-old widow lived her name was Jula. She was five feet tall, with blue eyes and her hair braided under a scarf on her head. We explained our situation. She was so sweet and kind. She offered us one room that we could share and told us we wouldn't have to pay much. We offered to help her clean her house and assist her with anything else she might need. She told us we were welcome to stay as long as we needed and allowed us the use of her stove. She was heaven-sent, cooking soup for us on cold nights when we worked so late. Finally, we had a place to sleep, with hot meals, a good mattress, clean sheets, and real pillows (not pillows made of straw). We thanked God for his grace and the opportunity he gave us to make a better life for ourselves. We fell in love with our landlady, Jula. She treated us so kindly, and she appreciated the company after living alone for so many years.

We worked Monday through Saturday for twelve hours every day. At times, we would work even longer on large orders or huge frames. Sometimes we worked on Sunday if we needed some extra money since the local church was not open every day, only on special days.

My workplace was a safety nightmare. We worked with chemicals without wearing masks or having ventilation fans, and many times, we left work feeling dizzy. Additionally, our boss wasn't the friendly type. He paid us late, and when he gave us our pay, he threw the money in front of us. We thanked him just the same. We didn't dare complain for fear of being fired. Once we got our first paychecks, we paid our landlady the monthly rent and used the rest of our earnings for food and clothes. At the time, I only had one pair of shoes, and my feet would get soaked every day as I sloshed through the snow on my way to work.

A couple months later, we heard from our father. He wrote to let us know how angry he was with me for leaving home without telling him and taking my sister with me. He said it was disrespectful of me but that he knew we were making a life for ourselves with supervision from Vera. He also wrote to tell us he was finally leaving Kosovo. He had purchased a small piece of land in a village called Dragobraca located about two hours away from Belgrade. He built a small home with the bricks he got from work. It started out as a small shelter and eventually became two more rooms. I was so happy to hear that my family had moved closer to me and my sister.

Those times were hard on him because my half-brothers and sisters expected my father to provide them with everything. My father had days when he would pick up leftover bread scraps from other employees during their lunch time, bag them up, and bring them home for my half-brothers, sisters, and his wife to eat. No matter what, he found a way to provide for his family.

Only Pair of Shoes I Owned

CHAPTER 10

Love from a Distance

In February 1980, I was walking home from the grocery store, when I spotted a tall, skinny young man about my age, with blue eyes and light-brown hair. He began to engage me in conversation. He went by the name of Dragan. He asked my name and wanted to know where I was from since he could see that I was new to the area. He was serving in the Yugoslavian Army and was home to spend time with his family. He talked about the new house his parents had built, next to the old home, which now served as a barn for their cattle. He went on his way, saying that he would like to see me again. I could tell that he was interested in me, and I was definitely falling for his charm.

The next day, we got together and swapped stories about our respective families. He swept me off my feet, promising me that he would protect me and take care of me. I believed everything he said. I didn't realize at the time that I was making a bad decision. He didn't tell me the truth when he said he only had three months left in the military. Six months later, he told me the same story, which should've been a red flag. Before he returned to his military unit, he introduced me to his parents, Jovan and Nada. They seemed very happy to meet me and welcomed me into their house. I was high on love and could finally see happiness in my future. He told me that he had a job waiting when he got out of the service in three months, which was again untruthful.

When he finally returned, I was happy to have my future husband back home. There was no engagement ring at this time since that is not a custom in Serbia. We were young and looking forward to spending time alone to get to know each other better. We laughed and had a good time.

Suddenly, we grew closer. We decided to move into his parents' house. This was common in Serbia. When you move into a house with a man, you are considered husband and wife. Out of respect, I called them mother and father because I lost my mother at a young age. I was very upset that I had to leave my sister Grozda behind. I built up the courage and asked my father-in-law if my sister could be allowed to stay with us on a temporary basis until she found a better paying job. He consented to this. My sister kept her job and helped out around the house. I was so thankful to God and my father-in-law for allowing this to happen and excited about moving into a new house, new life, new adventures, and having my sister with me. I couldn't have asked for better in-laws.

I soon began thinking the opposite. My mother-in-law made sure we had no privacy. Anytime we were alone behind closed doors, she had her ear to the door, listening to our conversations. We caught her doing this several times. I asked myself, why is she doing this? Could she be jealous of me, or did she think I was not good enough for her son? Did she forget what it was like to be in love?

It was becoming obvious that she didn't want her only son to be with me. I would get scolded for hugging him because it was "inappropriate" in her presence. However, when her daughter married and came for a visit, the newly-weds would hug and kiss in front of my mother-in-law. She said, "What a blessing to see a young couple in love." It was a good that she couldn't hear my thoughts.

Nada demanded that I needed to quit my job and stay at home to work on the farm, so I did. She was also scared that I would get involved with another man while her son was serving in the military. Just two months after quitting my job, I realized I'd made a terrible mistake. I milked the cows every morning and fed the cows, horse, pigs, chickens, ducks, and geese. I replaced the straw in the barn every day with a pitchfork, cleaned the barn, removed the cow manure, and transported it by wheelbarrow to the compost pile for the field and garden. I got down on my hands and knees and scrubbed the linoleum floors, did the laundry for the in-laws and husband (still by hand, as there were no washing machines), and helped prepare the meals. When the neighbors visited, they commented that my mother-in-law's house never looked so clean. These words made my mother-in-law very angry.

Nada was very tiny and frail. Her clothes were always falling off her, and she always wore a scarf. She wore two skirts and two sweaters most of the time to keep her clothes on. She had a noticeable mole on the corner of her upper lip and had dentures at the age of forty-six. Nada constantly complained about being sick and created an extraordinary amount of drama. She was a very bossy woman and barked orders at everyone else since she couldn't do much physical work around the property herself. However, when it came time to sell the cheese from the cow's milk at the market, she managed to find her strength. She wanted to maintain control of the money. Nada complained about everything I did around the house—nothing was good enough. Everything that I did, I was trying to please her. When my husband sent me letters from his military station, she became angry and jealous because he stopped writing her. Once she found out that I came from a poor family, her attitude toward me changed dramatically.

My father-in-law, Jovan, was five-foot, six-inches tall, had the hint of gray hair, and always wore pants even in the summertime. He was a good, hardworking person and always treated me well. First thing in the mornings, he went to the bakery and brought a loaf of fresh bread back to the house. He was never angry and always seemed to find a solution to every problem. Unlike my mother-in-law, he complimented the work I did around the home. I held out hope that my situation would improve.

My husband found a job as an auto mechanic, but he had a very poor work ethic. Sometimes he showed up; sometimes he didn't. At times, he would stay home and sleep until the middle of the day. He was finally fired when his boss discovered him sleeping on broken-down cardboard boxes at the job. He couldn't keep any job for long.

While my mother-in-law always had work for me, she never compelled her son to do any work around the house and provided him with money when needed it. I didn't want to argue with her since I was living under her roof, but every time I suggested to my husband that he look for a job, she told me I had no right to "boss him around." She did everything she could to stoke enmity and sow discord between my husband and me. She began taking my time away from him, asking me to do this or that. This drove a wall between Dragan and I. Everything I said and did was wrong. Of course, she never had a harsh word for her son. She had spoiled him his entire life, never provided a proper education, and even provided him with cigarettes at the age of sixteen. She never taught him the need to get a job or any responsibilities. Some mother, if you ask me.

One day, as I was milking the cows alongside my father-in-law, he told me he was planning to throw us a grand wedding party. I thanked my father-in-law for his kindness, but in my heart, I was afraid of getting married.

A week before the wedding, I fled to my sister Vera's apartment, crying and telling her that I didn't want to marry this man. He wouldn't work and was spoiled by his parents. My mother-in-law refused to let me have another job, except for on the farm. But my father-in-law had prepared for the wedding and sent out the invitations. I was torn. I told Vera and my brother-in-law that I could only see heartache in a future with this man. They convinced me that it would be shameful for me to back out since my father-in-law Jovan had spent so much time and money in preparing the wedding. This is the tradition in Serbia.

I questioned myself and asked God where He was and asked for his guidance. Why did I put myself in this situation? Would things ever improve? Every day, the situation between me and my mother-in-law and husband continued to deteriorate.

The month before we got married, I found out that I was eight weeks pregnant. I began to suffer from morning sickness, and I lost a great deal of weight. My mother-in-law was unfazed. She still expected the same level of work out of me.

I thought his parents would finally accept me as their daughter-in-law, and while his father did, his mother steadfastly refused. She wasn't happy to gain a daughter-in-law, but she was over the moon to have an extra person working on the farm.

Three months into my pregnancy, I became very thin. My OB/GYN prescribed me vitamin B6 for the morning sickness. I somewhat regained my appetite and got my strength back.

CHAPTER 11

Unhappily Ever After

When my husband found out that I'd fled to Vera's before the wedding, he promised that he would change. He would find a job, take care of me, and share some responsibilities. I allowed my future husband, Vera, and my brother-in-law, Nikola, to convince me to return home. On the way home, Dragan promised he'd take me to buy a wedding dress. A couple days later, we went to Belgrade and purchased a cheap dress that I was not happy with but wore anyways.

By the time we returned home, my mother-in-law was livid. The fear I felt earlier came rushing back. She did not like my choice of dress and had wanted to pick the dress for me. Her son spoke to her and calmed her down since he was the only one who could do so.

The big day finally came. I officially married their son in September of 1981. The wedding was a large affair, a huge celebration with lots of his family. On the day of the wedding, I had no one to help dress me, brush my hair, or apply my makeup. My mother-in-law certainly did not help me. We walked from our home to the justice of the peace to be married. We were unable to wed in a church because my husband was not baptized. My mother-in-law was not a religious woman. I waited for a sign from God to tell me what to do, but I received none. I did not want to marry this man and give him the title of my husband. I knew the situation with him, and his mother would never improve by simply changing my last name. After a long pause, I signed the documents and received my wedding ring. It was purchased along with wedding shoes by his uncle, which was Serbian tradition. As I signed the marriage license, I took a deep breath because I felt no happiness. My mother-in-law refused to take any pictures with me. Some of my own family attended, but they had no gifts to give. Since neither one of us had a job, we did not have a honeymoon.

When it came to "for better or for worse," my husband embraced the worse. I waited expectantly for all the changes my husband promised. None of them ever came to fruition. He would play cards with friends until the wee hours of the night, coming home at three or four o'clock in the morning. Very soon after, he began seeing other women, one being a waitress at the local restaurant. He lied about being married, and she left him when she found out the truth.

A month after our wedding, he became physically and emotionally abusive and very demanding. I had vision problems since I was a young girl, but he wouldn't allow me to wear glasses. He made fun of me when I wore them and ordered me to take them off. When I refused, he slapped me, calling me blind and telling me that he made a mistake when he married me. These words made me draw farther apart from him.

One night, he got angry with me for arguing with his mother about his sister Verica who was a nineteen-year-old diva. She never offered to help with daily chores like mopping the floor, wash her clothes, and attend to the farm animals. She would sleep in until 11:00 a.m. She lived with her family until she got married. This is the tradition as she can't afford to live on her own. When she got married, she came to the house weekly to take food and vegetables home with her. She refused to go out and pick vegetables and prepare meals for herself because she didn't want to damage her fingernails. Instead, my mother-in-law tried to send me out to get vegetables in the garden for her daughter. After so many times, I told her, "I'm not going." As punishment, my husband would leave me at the house alone all night long.

When he got angry, he would kick me out of our bed to stand in the empty hall with bare feet and thin pajamas. My whole body turned blue and shook from cold weather and the freezing cement I was sitting on while six months pregnant. I sat there, shivering and terrified. I prayed that God would save me and protect my unborn child. I hoped that once the baby came along, my husband would find a job and that his mother's opinion of me would improve. Of course, none of this transpired.

While I was pregnant, I told my husband that I needed more comfortable clothes that fit my growing stomach. Since my mother-in-law controlled the money in the house, my husband would have to ask her for some money.

Shortly after that conversation, we went into the kitchen. My husband was sitting on the couch and me on a wooden chair close by. My husband told his mother that I need some maternity clothes. She automatically refused. She told me to deal with what I had.

I replied, "You have no right to make such comments! I've earned the right to comfortable clothes working on your farm. You are becoming a drill sergeant!" As soon as the words came out of my mouth, my husband's hand came across my face. He hit me so hard that I fell out of the chair and onto the floor. It took me awhile to get my bearings back and realize what happened. I had bruises on both elbows, and my tail bone hurt enough that it had to have been fractured. God protected me and my unborn child by breaking my fall with his hands and saving both of us from my husband's wrath. "But I will restore you to health and heal your wounds" (Jeremiah 30:17).

I asked my husband why he refused to stand up for me. Could he not see that his mother was possessed and she was poisoning our marriage?

His father heard my hurtful words and became furious with me, simultaneously pulling out a knife from the kitchen drawer. He told me that he would show me why I don't talk to his wife that way under his roof. He looked possessed. He chased me with the knife, determined to hurt me.

I ran as fast as I could from the old house, setting my pain aside. My husband and I ran into the newly built house. We slammed the bedroom door and pushed with all our might to keep my father-in-law out. Both of us were surprised by his actions. My husband was actually protecting me for the first time. I was not strong enough to hold his father out by myself. I could feel my baby bouncing around. I feared for my life as well as my baby's. After ten minutes of fighting, banging on the door with his fist, and swearing, he finally cooled down. I began to have nightmares from this scenario. It replayed over and over in my mind.

I forgave my father-in-law because he had done good things for me and was only protecting his wife's honor. To this day, I light a candle in church and pray for his eternal life. God's power and love brought me through this danger.

CHAPTER 12

Baby on Board

Three months after this incident, I went into labor. My husband asked the neighbor Steva to drive me to the hospital in the middle of the night. In that time, Serbian hospitals did not have epidurals or any other type of painkillers. No one was allowed to visit other than the nurse who checked on me every hour. There was only one nurse for a dozen screaming, expecting mothers. In May 1982, at 9:30 a.m. and after ten hours of excruciating contractions, my beautiful daughter, Jelena, came into the world.

I was so excited for my baby girl! At that time, we did not have ultrasounds to find out the gender of the baby before it was born. I immediately fell in love with her. The photographer came around to take mother and child photos. Since I didn't have any money, the photographer took them for free. I had two other visitors: my husband and, quite surprisingly, my mother-in-law. When she visited, her first question wasn't to inquire about my well-being. Instead, she asked if the baby had all her fingers and toes. I suppose she asked because she knew how many times my husband had slapped or beaten me and that she was responsible for so many of the quarrels between my husband and me. She didn't want to feel responsible for any birth defects.

My beautiful baby girl brought me so much joy! I told her how much I loved her and that I would never let her grow up experiencing the same hard times I had grown up with. I covered her with kisses and thanked God for giving me such a beautiful gift.

Six days after giving birth, I left the hospital with Jelena. Having a baby brought a whole host of new responsibilities. In addition to taking care of Jelena, I had to take care of the chores on the farm. I didn't have as much time with her as I would have liked since I had to tend to my mother-in-law's demands. I put a radio beside Jelena's bed so she could hear voices around her as she slept.

My husband was a heavy smoker, and he smoked without regard for the baby. His mother would supply him with cigarettes since he didn't have the money. He never helped with any of the child-rearing responsibilities. Having a baby also gave my mother-in-law a whole raft of new things to criticize. More than once, she would scream and yell at me as I was breastfeeding my daughter. She'd tell me that if I held the baby, I would spoil her. Apparently, she thought I was spending too much time washing diapers and tending to other baby-related tasks. She also would not allow me to purchase clothing for myself or Jelena.

My father-in-law always thanked me for washing his clothes, and he was not afraid to criticize his son for his laziness. He reiterated the need for my husband to find a job and pitch in with the chores. I'll never forget the day we all had to work in the cornfield. My husband, being the malingerer that he was, claimed that he didn't feel well. He faked and rolled around on the floor in pain, deserving an Academy Award for his performance, crying that he needed to stay home. Halfway to the field, the old farm truck broke down. My father-in-law tried to fix the truck but had no success. He told me to walk back home to fetch my husband and they would watch over Jelena. When I arrived at the house, my husband was nowhere to be found. I went to look at his favorite place at the restaurant, found him chatting up a waitress and having coffee. I was not surprised to find him there. I told him that his father needed his assistance in fixing the truck. He was not in a hurry. He eventually turned up, hours later. Fortunately, my father-in-law managed to get the truck started.

When I lived in Serbia, I was treated as a second-class citizen. A man could take whatever he wanted from his wife without asking or giving back. Women were expected to stay at home and care for the children while the man went to work…except that did not happen in my marriage. The first part was true for us, but apparently the part about the man going to work was just a suggestion for him. I was more of a slave, not a wife. My husband was free to come and go as he pleased. My opinions did not matter. He cursed me, made nasty comments about my deceased mother, and was completely heartless.

As I mentioned previously, neither my husband nor his family never attended church services. The church in our village was only opened for funerals, weddings, and holy days. My in-laws never said grace at mealtime or thanked God for anything. I prayed for God's help, hoping that He had not forgotten about me. How much longer would I have to wait to find happiness when it looked like there was no end in sight to the suffering?

Eight months after I gave birth to Jelena, I found out I was once again pregnant.

CHAPTER 13

Surprise, Surprise!

When I told my husband I was pregnant again, he swore up and down that this time he would really, truly change, promises that proved once again to be completely empty. I knew this type of sudden change would be unlikely.

My mother-in-law was enraged at the news of my pregnancy. She demanded that I have to end my pregnancy. For days, she drilled into me constantly that having the baby would be a terrible mistake and that I needed to "take care of it" before it was too late. I did not listen to her advice.

My husband made an outward appearance of trying to change course for a few months. He played with our daughter, helped his father on the farm, and stopped slapping me. Occasionally, my father would come to visit. He did not like my husband or my in-laws. He knew about the physical and verbal abuse. He advised me to leave my husband, telling me that he would help me.

When I was seven months pregnant, my husband returned to his standard practices. I knew it wouldn't be long. I had nowhere to go for help but prayed to God to guide me. I was completely lost. There were no food stamps, welfare, or domestic abuse shelters where I could escape from my husband and mother-in-law. The morning sickness made my pregnancy difficult. I continued to milk six cows, butcher chickens, work in the fields, and prepare meals. While milking the cows, I found it difficult with my growing belly. Manure-covered cow tails would hit me in the face as the cows tried to swat away flies. I was also worried that the cow, in its irritation with the biting flies, would kick over the bucket, wasting our precious milk and income.

I parked Jelena in a stroller in front of the barn doors, worrying that she would be trampled by a cow who suddenly got it in her mind to bolt out of the barn doors. Many times, my seventy-six-year-old neighbor, Desa, came into the barn and sat on a wooden stool by my daughter's stroller to keep her company. She used a leafy branch to wave away flies from her face. She was very caring and helpful, and I repaid her by baking her cookies and cakes.

I continued to work up until I gave birth. My father-in-law would help me with the heavy lifting if he were around, but even with my very pregnant belly and swollen legs, my husband gave me no help. In September 1983, I went into labor while washing clothes that day.

My son Alexandar was born at 11:30 p.m. Once again, I was alone in the delivery room, wearing a hospital gown so full of holes it looked as though it had been used for target practice. This time, my labor only lasted four hours. I was so happy to hold my son in my arms, and I fell in love with him just as I did with my daughter sixteen months earlier. I spent three days in the hospital. This time I received no visitors. Each day I waited for someone to walk through the door, at least my husband. Other mothers had husbands and new grandparents bearing gifts, flowers, and hugs, all of them filled with joy. As lonely as I was, I knew that my God was with me, as he promises in Deuteronomy 31:6, "He will never leave or forsake you."

After three days, the doctor cleared me to go home because the hospital didn't have enough beds. Since we didn't have a phone, I couldn't call my husband, so I used what little change I had in my purse to send a postcard to my husband telling him he needed to pick us up. My sister-in-law Verica and her husband picked me up from the hospital. My husband told me that he was unable to come pick me up since he was so busy on the farm (so he said). He also said he was disappointed to have a son. He had no interest in how his son and I were doing. Unlike my husband, my father-in-law was delighted to have a grandson who would carry his last name. The first thing my mother-in-law said was that he didn't look like anyone in her family, what with his black hair and dark complexion. He looked more like my family. Her words were very hurtful to me. I put my mother-in-law's hateful comments out of my mind and did not engage in further conversation with her about my baby. On the other hand, Jelena was overjoyed to see me return from the hospital with her new baby brother.

His hair and complexion began to lighten after three weeks. When my son turned three, his mother-in-law's wish came true. My son's hair turned a curly blond, his eyes were blue, and he looked more like her own family.

Shortly after I gave birth, I found out about my husband's continuing infidelity. He spent all day with another young woman, not returning home until 3:00 a.m. While I cared for myself and my babies, he continued to be unfaithful. I began to ignore him and everyone else, concentrating my efforts on taking care of my children. My kids did not have fancy toys or clothes when they were small, but I gave them all my time and love.

As Alexandar grew, by the time he was six months, Alek was constantly crawling to the point that he wore holes in the knees of all his pants. At eight months, he started walking on his own. He followed his grandpa around the farm, wanting to do everything he did. He liked to be busy and work with his hands. Grandpa had an old bicycle in the barn. Alek took the entire bicycle apart and put it back together on several occasions. To this day, he still likes to work with his hands.

Once while Alek was outside trying to change his underwear with a clean pair from the clothesline, he was assailed by a rooster, who launched an attack on his most sensitive areas. In fact, that rooster seemed to know just where to attack every time. The rooster began attacking other family members as well, jumping on my mother-in-law's back as she bent down. The rooster ended up in the stew pot.

My father was the only family member to visit me and try to help me out of the mess I was in. He never had much in his life, but he did everything in his power to give me a better future. My father didn't have an education, so he had to take any job he could find. As he was working as a construction worker, he fell off a structure and broke some ribs. He never sought medical attention. As a result, he experienced internal bleeding and complications from the accident. This, along with many years of smoking, took a toll on him. He soon developed lung cancer. By the time he got to a doctor, it was too late. I was constantly praying to God to put his healing hands on my father. When I went to visit him in the hospital during his chemotherapy treatments, he was more worried about me than his illness. The lung cancer was very aggressive. Six months after his diagnosis, he fell asleep with the Lord on March 21, 1986, at only fifty-six years of age.

The night before his passing, I had yet another nightmare involving a snake. In this dream, a snake bit me on the left hand as I slept in my bed. I woke up screaming and turned on the light. Once again, the dream was so real, I checked my hand for bite marks. I thanked God when I realized it was just a nightmare.

The next morning, the neighbor knocked on our door at 6:00 a.m. to tell me that I had a phone call from my family. We did not have a phone and used their phone for emergencies. It was my half-sister Vera phoning to notify me of my father's passing.

His death was very painful, and I wish he was still alive to see how much better my life is now. His final resting place is 250 miles from the cemetery where my mother and grandparents are buried since he sold our original house. My father's coffin was provided by his employer since he was the only provider for his home. His death was devastating for all of us, especially my youngest siblings. My dad was the only provider they ever had since my stepmother never held a job. With most of my family living so far away, I had few people to lean on for support, except God.

Four years after the birth of my daughter, I was still alone, with no help, no money, and forbidden to make my own decisions. I could not continue to live my life like this. I ignored my mother-in-law's rules and started going back to church. God opened my eyes to realize that my first priority is to take care of myself and my children. He strengthened me as Isaiah 41:10 says he will: "So do not fear, for I am with you; do not be dismayed, for I am your God. I will strengthen you and help you; I will uphold you with my righteous right hand."

My sister Grozda was living and working in Austria at the time. I traveled there twice to stay with her and look for work. I did not have any luck either time. Each time I had to return home, I felt hopeless and sad, knowing what waited for me each time I came back. After returning from Austria the second time, I began to look for work close to home and find daycare for my children. I found a job six miles from home making jewelry, keychains, and candles. It didn't pay much, but I was happy to have a job that paid for daycare and food and ultimately kept me away from my mother-in-law's daily drama.

My husband and father-in-law demanded that I hand over my paycheck. His reasoning was that I owed him after living under his roof for so many years. I did not mind giving my father-in-law money since I knew it would go toward food and necessities. However, I was not giving my low-down, lazy husband a dime of my hard-earned paycheck.

The few times I gave my husband money to pay for the children's daycare, he used the money to buy gifts for his girlfriend. I found out what he'd done when the daycare sent notes home with Jelena, demanding payment for the monthly bill. When I told them that my husband paid it, they let me know that wasn't the case.

I woke up every day at 5:00 a.m. to dress Jelena and Alek, drop them off at daycare, and go to work. My husband stayed out late every night and slept late every morning. My morning routine was much more difficult in the winter, trudging through the snow and cold by foot with the children. I continued to work during the days and late into the evening.

Falling into an everyday routine, I realized that I had lapsed in my faith. I knew I needed to return to the church and have my children baptized. Neither my husband nor mother-in-law approved of this, but I didn't care. My children's salvation was more important than their opinions. When I spoke with the priest about baptizing my children, he informed me that my husband would need to be baptized first.

There were many arguments, but after much prayer on my part, miraculously, my husband agreed to be baptized with his mother's approval. This increased my confidence that God was looking out for me. When you are baptized, Orthodox faithful believe that a person is reborn again and belongs to Christ. Baptism is the door through which we enter the family of God. It is the first mystery of the Orthodox faith. Renounce sin and Satan. They are a child of God and of life eternal.

CHAPTER 14

Bad Guy

One night, my husband returned home uncharacteristically early to tell me that he was no longer in love with me. This came as no great shock. I told him he could go anywhere he pleased with his girlfriend, but I informed him that under no condition would he get my children. I refused to allow them to grow up with a stepmother. My husband demanded that I leave immediately, or he would beat me every day until I did. My father-in-law stood up for me and told his son that I would stay in the house with my children. If my husband wasn't happy, he was welcome to live with his girlfriend anywhere else but not under his roof. Once my mother-in-law found out that her son was abandoning me for a woman ten years younger than me, her demeanor toward me became much friendlier.

One day my husband came up to me, demanding to know when I was leaving. I told him I wouldn't desert my children, and he punched me in the jaw. I was bleeding so severely, I thought he'd broken all my teeth. My shirt was covered in blood, and my head felt as if it was bursting from the pain. I walked out of the house and down the street, looking for a phone to call the police. I thought if they saw the state I was in, they would have to do something. I went to the closest restaurant and asked if I could use their phone. The lady there warned me not to call the police. According to her, I just needed to work things out with my husband. Besides, she said the police would do nothing about it since I was his wife.

When I returned home, I tried to enter the darkened room where my children were sleeping, only to discover that my husband had locked me out. I had to sit on the front steps until morning in my blood-soaked clothes with an aching split lip. I rested my pounding head on my hands against the wall. I tried to sleep but had no success with so much stress and pain.

When I finally got into the house, I washed away the vibrant blood, but I couldn't do anything about the darkened bruises and split lip that were so glaringly obvious. In the morning, I took my children to daycare and went to work. Everyone at work was immediately concerned. I told them I fell in the shower and hurt myself, but nobody bought it since the whole village knew of my situation. My boss was very supportive and kind. He hated to see me suffer for as long as I had. He allowed me to earn extra money for myself and my children.

I prayed constantly, but I felt discouraged not seeing any immediate change. My husband was beating me nearly every day. The day before I left forever, I told my father-in-law that I couldn't take any more. He said that I could go anywhere, and he would take care of the children until

I found a place to live. He told me that his son was so angry, he was sure he would eventually destroy me. The ensuing night was one of the most terrifying nights of my life and served as the final straw in the decision to leave my husband.

My husband returned home around 3:00 a.m. after visiting his girlfriend. I was sleeping with my children in our bedroom. I heard the gate open into our yard, and I worried what he would do when he saw me, still there. The brown metal gate brought fear every night, like a wave over my body when I would hear it screeching. This meant he was home. He flipped on the overhead light and demanded I move over to make room for him in the bed. He lit a cigarette and began smoking in the bedroom where the children and I were sleeping. The acrid smell of cigarette smoke permeated everything in the room. Our clothing, skin, bedsheets, and even the walls all smelled of smoke.

He wanted me to turn around so he could show me a large, sharp hunting knife with a rainbow-colored handle laying on his chest. He asked if I wanted him to kill me or should I kill myself?

I was in such a state of shock from that ultimatum. I prayed desperately. I attempted to be as nice as I could to avoid angering him. I whispered softly that nobody would be killing anybody, and I'll leave first thing in the morning. I began to shake. My legs wobbled and I thought my heart would explode. I was terrified for my children. I walked out of the room and went to the room where his parents slept. I told them what their son had said and explained that I would need to leave as soon as possible. Since my own parents were gone, I would need their help watching the children. I went to another room and locked the door behind me. I spent the rest of the night praying and making plans for my escape, wondering how I would survive and ensure no harm would come to my children. It was a very difficult plan to be comfortable with, but it had to be done. I had nowhere to go.

The next morning, I dressed my children with a new-found determination. My father-in-law agreed to watch the children while I was gone. I spent all day looking with fire in my soul but couldn't find anyone who would rent me a room. I returned home at 10:00 p.m. to find the door blocked with an old stove. Angry and determined, I forced my way inside. He was sitting in his chair, smoking as usual, and told me that he wouldn't change his mind about me having to leave. I had no suitcases, so I stuffed everything I owned into a few thin plastic grocery bags picked up from the street. I wanted to hug my children, but they were asleep, and my husband pushed me against the door, not wanting to start another fight.

I watched them, heartbroken, with tears streaming down my eyes and left. I knew that I couldn't spend one more night with my husband. Nor could I take them with me since I had nowhere to go. I was unaware that hidden behind a stack of bricks in front of the house was my husband's pregnant girlfriend, Violeta, waiting for me to leave. As I was closing the gate, I saw her strut into the house. She moved in immediately after I left. I finally realized why my husband wanted me gone so quickly.

I felt God telling me to just go, that my children would be fine, and that I would eventually get them back. I did not want my children to grow up with a stepmother.

After eight years, the torture and abuse were finally over. I walked to the bus station late at night. I was terrified of being attacked by roaming, rabid dogs. I planned to spend the night at my best friend Yoka and coworker's house. I arrived at the bus station shortly after 11:00 p.m. The bus station was located in front of my neighbor's house, and she saw me through the window, alone with my plastic bags. She asked where I was going, so I told her. She let me know that the last bus had already gone and would not return until 7:00 a.m. She then invited me to spend the night in her house and catch the bus the next morning. I thanked her for her generosity and took her up on her offer. She was heaven-sent.

I realized then that God was still looking out for me. I followed her to a nice, clean bedroom. She asked if I was hungry. I thanked her and told her I had no appetite. I tried to sleep, but I was too nervous and sick to my stomach. I was worried about my children and how my husband's girlfriend would treat them. Would she attempt to brainwash them against me? I cried all night in despair.

I woke up around 6:30 and readied myself for the 7:00 a.m. bus. The neighbor named Zora was already up and about, telling me that she'd prayed for me. I thanked her for her generosity and prayers and let her know that I would never forget her. I prayed that God would reward her double in return.

CHAPTER 15

Moving On

When I arrived at the bus station, I entered the bus without a proper ticket. The bus driver drove me to my destination. Thankfully, I did not get caught. I walked the rest of the way to my friend Yoka's house.

When I arrived, she welcomed me inside and let me know that she would help me find a place. She knew of an older lady who lived alone, close to my job. When we arrived at the lady's apartment, we met a frail eighty-year-old woman with dark clothing and a scarf over her gray hair by the name of Milka. She was diabetic, and her legs were swollen, so she spent most of her time on the couch. She was happy to have someone to keep her company. After extensive apartment hunting, she told me that I could live with her. She wouldn't charge me much because she needed help going to the grocery store and doing household tasks. I gladly accepted her offer, knowing that I finally had a safe place to sleep.

She allowed me to use an old bicycle in the garage for transportation. She was very easy to please and always complimented my hard work and cleanliness. The little room that I slept in was empty and had enough cracks in the ceiling and walls that made me worry about it caving in on me. There was also no bed, so I slept on a sofa in her room that night.

My husband's relative, Jasna, offered to sell me her couch that she no longer needed. After church one day, I went to her house to buy the old couch. I did not expect the couch to be stored in the attic. It was full of dust. The back was ripped off, and it had holes in the cushions. I paid much more than I planned to. I cleaned it up and slept on it anyways.

In the morning, my friend Dragica asked if I wanted to earn some extra money helping an older man on his farm. Of course, I agreed. That morning, Milka gave me bread and filled a plastic bottle of water for me. My friend took an onion and cheese with her that she shared with me during our lunch break. We talked about kids, and she encouraged me to be patient because God had a plan for me. My friend and I ended up working in his cornfield all day. It was a hot day of sweating profusely. Our backs hurt from bending over and hoeing weeds, but at the end of the day, the farmer was delighted. He paid us well and told us what an excellent job we did taking care of his cornfield. We let him know that we would gladly work for him anytime he needed us.

My children were constantly on my mind. Were they being fed and bathed? Did they miss me or ask about me? One day after I left home, Jasna visited me at work. She informed me that my husband had brought his pregnant girlfriend into his parents' house. This was not news to me. My blood ran cold. My heart was broken for my children. My father-in-law told me that a week after she moved in, her mother came around to visit. For the first time, she found out that her daughter was pregnant by a married man with two children. The woman was so disappointed and angry with her daughter. She demanded to know if her daughter was responsible for destroying a marriage and separating a mother from her two children.

I would visit my children when my husband and his girlfriend were away. My father-in-law kept me in the loop about the kids. I found out from my father-in-law that my fears were true. I never expected my husband's girlfriend to be a suitable stepmother since she was so young and immature. She did not take care of my kids but would lock them in a room for hours on end until she returned from coffee and chatting with her friends. She never attempted to make any connection with my children at all. Every week, my father-in-law would come to my work to tell me how badly she treated them. That made my life more miserable, and it was hard to concentrate. At the time, Yugoslavia had no mechanism for reporting spousal or child abuse. People just had to live with it.

While I was still married and working at my job, I received health insurance through my employer. After leaving my husband, I had him removed from my health insurance. When he found out, he was angry and came to my workplace to argue with me. He demanded to know why I'd dropped him from the policy. I let him know that he had no right to be on my policy after the way he had abused and discarded me. He'd finally found a stable job working as an auto mechanic in Belgrade, but his health insurance wasn't as good as mine.

I wanted to legally divorce him as quickly as possible. I took a bus to the justice building in *Pecinci*. When I was walking the city streets, a well-dressed gentleman, about forty-five years old, stopped me and asked if he could help me. I guess he noticed me looking around, dazed and confused, not knowing the area I was in. I told him my situation. He just so happened to work where I needed to go. I realized God had placed this man in my path after getting off the bus. As we walked to his office, he wanted to know my reason for wanting a divorce. I explained everything, then asked him what the cost would be. After hearing my story, he shook his head in disbelief. He offered to help me fill out the paperwork and file it at no cost. The next step was to mail the paperwork and wait for the court to call us both.

A month later, we received our respective letters. We arrived at the courtroom at the same time. My husband was furious, cursing at me, demanding to know why I was rushing a divorce from him, as if this was a surprise. My tears spilled forth, thinking of my children.

The judge asked him if he wanted to work things out for the sake of our children. My husband flat-out refused. He wanted to continue living with his girlfriend and have nothing else to do with me.

I was delighted to hear this. After telling the judge where I lived and my current income, in contrast to my husband's situation and support, he ordered custody of my children to my husband. My husband was extremely displeased at being held responsible for the care of his own children. However, I had visitation rights each weekend, and he was not allowed to touch me.

I was elated that my eight years of misery was finally over. Six months after my divorce, I read in the newspaper that the very same gentleman, my saving grace sent from God, who helped me file for divorce at no cost, was killed by a car as he crossed the street. My heart shattered.

After the divorce, my father-in-law came to my work and notified me that Dragan's girlfriend had hit my son across the face with a wooden spoon and left bruises on his cheeks. She spanked my children anytime they didn't listen or follow her rules. I was devastated, and my heart was ready to explode. I didn't wait for my father-in-law to finish the story. I told my boss I had an emergency with my children and would return shortly. I got on my bicycle and pedaled furiously to the house, gaining more anger the closer I came. My adrenaline kicked in. Nothing was going to slow me down or get between me and my children. I left my father in-law far behind in my dust.

I was at my in-laws' house in fifteen minutes. Violeta was standing alone on the porch as I pulled in. I asked her where my children were and told her I wanted to see them. When I walked into the house, I asked, "Why are there bruises on my son's face?"

I informed her that she could spank her own offspring but that she had no right to touch mine. She looked shocked, wondering how I'd found out. When I got inside, I found my children alone in a room. I asked my son what had happened to his face, and he responded that he had fallen on a stack of bricks. I hugged him tightly. I told him I knew that it wasn't true. He was so frightened that he stuck to his story.

I turned to the girlfriend and told her that if she ever did this to my child again, she would live to regret it. The children told me that in addition to her, their father would spank them with a belt when he came home from work. I was at a loss.

The next day, I told Dragan that his girlfriend had no right to beat, starve, or to lock my children alone in a room. He finally took his girlfriend to find an apartment in the city, leaving our children behind with his parents. I was so thankful for his parents at this time. While Dragan didn't bother to maintain contact with his children, I maintained contact with his parents.

House of Landlord Milka

CHAPTER 16

New Start

Every Sunday morning, I rode my bike to church. I knew if I was going to take my children back, I needed a stronger connection with my heavenly Father. I was happy in church, although there were not many people my age. Being new and all alone in the church was not easy. I spent a lot of time at the church praying to God to guide my path.

The priest was divorced, and his wife had custody of their two children. The older people in the church did not know my situation and began gossiping. Members began saying that the only reason I came to church was because I was in love with the priest. Obviously, none of their gossip was true. I came to pray for God's help and my children's wellbeing.

One Sunday after church as I rode my bike home, I ran out of energy. I couldn't pedal the bike anymore. I suddenly felt extreme weakness in my legs. I could only push it slowly along as I walked home. My hair had been falling out to the point I feared I would be bald. I was terribly thin, and my circulation was so poor that my feet were always cold. After I told a friend about the physical pain and my lack of energy, she pointed out that I needed to eat fresh fruit and vegetables as well as get more sleep, and my health would improve. She was right, of course. My diet had taken a hard hit. I wasn't getting nearly the amount of proper nutrition that I needed.

After church, I would pick up my children and bring them to my house. We spent quality time together as I prepared meals for them. I had no furniture for them to sleep on, so I asked my boss for an advance on my paycheck to purchase furniture. He helped me purchase the furniture, and I paid him back as I was able. I bought a small couch, small refrigerator, and a stove with the loan so that I could prepare better meals for my kids.

A year after my divorce, my daughter Jelena began first grade. Her teacher Rosa repeatedly called her father for three months, but he could never find the time to meet with her, so she finally called me. I met with her and Jelena at the school and found out that Jelena needed help with her homework. The teacher said Jelena talked about me constantly and told her how sad she was.

In first grade, Jelena ran away from home several times by boarding a bus alone and showing up at my workplace. Luckily, nothing bad ever happened to her. She was stopped by villagers who asked her where she was going. She told them she was going to see her mother at work, and one was kind enough to give her a ride to my workplace.

One day at school, Jelena was chased by a classmate. She missed the handle that opened the door and pushed right through the glass, slicing her wrist. She bled severely. The school notified her grandparents who inexplicably brought her to me instead of the emergency room. I was in shock and ran to my neighbor for a ride to the hospital. They gave her stitches at the hospital and used no anesthetic. Her screams were nerve-wracking. I cried as much as she did. As soon as the doctor finished, Jelena's father showed up. The doctor told us that she would need to stay close to the hospital since she'd lost so much blood. They also wanted her close by in case there were any other complications. Since her father's house was closer to the hospital, she stayed with him. I worried with her being out of my sight. He was not the best at communicating about her healing process, which made me worry more.

When Jelena stayed with her stepmother during her recovery, she grabbed her injured arm in an attempt to get her attention. My ex-husband's girlfriend didn't like the idea of Jelena spending the week with them and having to take on any additional responsibility.

Jelena's teacher Rosa called me when her father did not respond to her calls. When I arrived at the school, Jelena was upset and crying. She didn't want to go back to her grandparents' house. The next day, Dragan showed up in front of my place of business. I decided to hear what he had to say, so I walked out. He wanted to know why I was showing up at Jelena's school. When I approached him to explain, he punched me in the face. I fell down, dizzy and bleeding, with a newly busted lip. While still laying on the ground, he walked away, ordering me to never return to the school again. This caused trouble between Jelena and her grandparents.

My coworkers came to help me up and gave me a bag of ice for my lip. My lip was so swollen that I couldn't eat or drink for several days. After this, I had trouble sleeping and was plagued by nightmares. I was always afraid he would return, but it was the last time he ever had the opportunity to hit me. I could never understand why he was like this. I worked hard, respected his parents, and did everything they asked. I gave them my paychecks and paid for the food I ate when I lived with them. Nothing was ever good enough.

There was a small mirror surrounded by a silver plastic frame hanging on the wall in Milka's, my landlord's, house. One morning while brushing my hair, the brush slipped and hit the mirror, knocking it to the floor. The mirror shattered. As I swept the glass off the floor, I apologized over and over, then promised to replace it. I was so upset, thinking I would have seven more years of bad luck. The mirror breaking was the straw that finally broke the camel's back. At church, my emotions came out like a flood. I couldn't quit crying. I missed my kids, had less work, less money, no other jobs, false accusations, and had no help from nobody. All these things had been adding up over time. After my employer filed for bankruptcy, I had to sell my furniture to make ends meet, and I was hanging on by a thread. I was alone and had placed my last dinar in the offering plate. I was alone and had placed my last dinar in the offering plate. I knelt down in front of God and told Him it was the last chance to help me.

He tells us in Psalm 50:15, "Call on me in the day of trouble; I will deliver you, and you will honor me."

After an hour of praying, I went back to the apartment to lie down. I was lying on my back on the stained mattress. The room was so cold, I hugged myself, tucking my work-chapped fingers under my arms. Misty puffs of air hung over my head with every breath I took. I closed my eyes and prayed that God would save me.

Five minutes later, I saw fluffy white clouds on my ceiling, with God sitting on them with his white hair and beard. The clouds came toward me, closer and closer. When I thought the clouds would touch me, I opened my eyes, lifted my hands in the air, and shouted, "Please accept me."

He began drifting further and further back to where I could no longer see him. I felt a slight sense of relief. I felt like this was the end of my struggles.

I felt as though Almighty God wanted to speak to me. It looked exactly like the icon of the Trinity that I received from the priest at my church, along with the Bible he had given me. At that moment, everything disappeared into the air. I was relieved of the despair I felt earlier in church. I stood up with the realization that I had experienced a powerful miracle (one of many more to come).

I walked to my sweet Grandma Milka's room to tell her about the experience I just had. She believed me and was happy for me. She then told me that while I was at church, one of our neighbors came around looking for me.

The same neighbor came by my workplace during the last week of March in 1990 to tell me of a woman who owned a business in Germany. She came to Serbia looking for cocktail waitresses and a nanny for her child. Everyone in the village introduced me to her, telling her that I was a hard worker, that she would never regret hiring me. They really talked me up.

As I spoke with the woman and her husband, she asked if I had my passport and divorce papers. I had both of these things, along with every other piece of needed documentation. She offered me the job and gave me the option of driving to Germany with her family or taking the train. Since I didn't have money for the train, I opted to ride with them.

I came home and spoke with Milka, telling her the broken mirror turned out to be good luck. She was sad that I was leaving but happy for the brighter future ahead. She wished me the best of luck, and I hoped this was the end of my struggles.

I quickly packed my clothes in green and yellow plastic bags and readied my documentation. I gave away my refrigerator and stove to my neighbor since she'd told me about the job in Germany. After all, I couldn't take it with me. After two years of dreaming and praying, everything I had hoped for was finally coming to fruition. God picked me up and guided me toward a better future.

I rode my bicycle to my former in-laws to tell them what was happening. My former father-in-law was standing in the street, speaking with the neighbors. I told him about the job opportunity in Germany. I needed to check it out before taking the kids with me and asked if he would be willing to look after them until I come for them. I promised to send money for food, clothes, and school supplies for the children.

With a joyful smile, he immediately told me yes, to not worry and just go. Once everything was in order, I could come get my children.

I was overjoyed to hear his promise. Their care for my kids and the fact that I never went hungry in their house are the two positive things I can say about them. I left for Germany that day. Even though I didn't have time to say goodbye to my children, my former grandfather recommended that I don't go to school to cause an emotional scene. I was happy knowing that after twenty-nine years of struggling, the heartache was behind me.

Church Where I Worshiped God   Gods First Appearance

CHAPTER 17

Germany

I arrived in Germany on April 3, 1991Everything was different. Different houses, apartments, stores, and more importantly, a different language.

I helped my employer around her home, doing household tasks and babysitting her child. My boss was Serbian, so it was not hard for me to communicate with her. She allowed me and a Polish woman to live in her dark, dusty storage room. I couldn't complain because this was the first time I ever had a running shower with hot water and a washer/dryer for my clothes. I made a lot more money at this job than I had ever made in my entire life. I was able to send enough money back home to support my children and for my former mother-in-law to purchase a washing machine, making laundry a much easier task.

As soon as I began thinking everything was good, I started to worry about my children. I prayed unceasingly for the safety of my children, of my family, and everyone else in Serbia as war began. I called my children at least every other day to make sure everything was okay.

When I spoke with their grandfather, Jovan, he told me that Dragan, his girlfriend, and their child went on vacation to the beach, leaving Jelena and Alexandar behind. Instead, he sent them a postcard. My former father-in-law was so upset with his son, asking him why he left his other two children behind.

My ex's only answer was that he was embarrassed to be with them. Their grandfather burned the postcard in the woodstove, never allowing my children to see it. By now, my ex owned a very successful auto repair business, but he never provided any monetary support to our children or participated in their lives. They never even received a single birthday gift from him. In fact, the only gift I ever received from my ex-husband during the long eight years together was a pair of stockings and a measly bar of soap.

Six months after living in Germany, Jelena's grandfather called to tell me she was very ill with stomach issues and a high fever. I went to the German pharmacy and purchased medication based on their recommendation. That night, I boarded a bus to Serbia. After traveling all night, I finally arrived and went to see my children. They were so happy, and their grandparents allowed me to stay with them.

While I was in Serbia, I took a train with my brother-in-law since it was dangerous for women to travel alone. We went to Kosovo to retrieve my birth certificate, not knowing I'd need my shot records in the future when I would leave Germany for the US. While in Kosovo, I took the opportunity to visit my mother's and grandparents' graves for the very last time.

After two days of medication, Jelena was feeling better. My half-sister, Vera, called and suggested we plan a three-day beach vacation with our children in Montenegro. We traveled through the dark night on a train, all of us sleeping on the dirty floors of the aisle way since we had no reservations. We had a wonderful time relaxing on the sandy beach, breathing in the fresh air before returning home. My kids deserved a break since their father left them behind on his own beach vacation.

I finally had to say goodbye and board the bus back to Germany. It was a sharp, stabbing pain that I had to leave my children behind. I had nowhere for them to stay. I needed a little bit more time to get my job, home, and life in order. I waved goodbye out of the dusty window of the bus, holding rushing tears back as my children cried and waved from the curbside of the bus station.

CHAPTER 18

New Life, New Love

After a month working as a cocktail waitress, I met the love of my life. There was a handsome uniformed man across the room. When we locked eyes, we connected immediately. It was that "love at first sight" feeling. God sent me the person I didn't know I was looking for. There was an obvious strong connection that we both felt.

He made his way over to me, ordered a drink, and offered to buy me one as well.

Since my shift was almost over, I agreed.

He spoke no German and certainly no Serbian. I spoke very little English. Our main form of communication that night was through the drawing of pictures. We asked each other about our lives through pictures. I found out his name was Larry, and he was in the United States Air Force. As soon as we met, I told him about my two children because I wanted him to be completely honest with me about his own situation. I was worried after having divorced a man who constantly lied to me. My new love told me truthfully that he had an ex-wife back in the United States but no children. His marriage had fallen apart after four years, and he was gun shy about being in another relationship, fearing that all women would be like his ex-wife.

After we found out that we were both divorced and single, we grew closer. After a very short time, he asked me to be his girlfriend. I gladly accepted. He visited me at work and took me to nice places. It felt good to be with a loving man. Of course, communication was complicated. I wanted to know more about him. I went to the city in search of a Serbian-English dictionary. I learned some of the basic romantic phrases, including "darling," "when are you coming to visit me again," and "I love you."

He wanted to live together to find out if we were compatible. After six months of dating, we moved in together. It was the happiest time of my life. For the first time, I had a man who cared for me, told me he loved me and that I was beautiful, and showed me affection. He gave me the first birthday present I ever received on my thirtieth birthday. Two months after moving in, he told me that I didn't have to work. He gave me money to send to my children, and every day, we overcame the language barrier just a little more.

After quitting my job, we eventually began to travel around Europe together, visiting Switzerland, the Netherlands, Belgium, England, Austria, and France. My darling was a great organizer and navigator. We enjoyed every minute. The trip from the Netherlands to England was my first trip by boat. I was amazed at how knowledgeable he was with his finances and how well he did at his job at Ramstein Air Base. He was a very well-respected senior non-commissioned officer (SNCO).

Shortly after I moved in with him in October, my darling had to attend the SNCO Academy for two months in Montgomery, Alabama. Since I did not have a driver's license I stayed behind in Germany and babysat six children ages one to six to have some sort of income. I wanted to have a little extra money so that my darling didn't have to pay for everything.

He wrote to me every day during the two months he was gone. I missed him terribly and looked forward to each letter. It took me a day or two to look through the dictionary word-by-word to translate every letter. I was having to learn German and English at the same time. I continued to improve my English so I could write him back, of course. Writing one letter in English took me two days!

I have strongly believed that God has guided my path since the moment I was born. All the desperate prayers were finally answered, and he sent me to Germany for a very exact reason. Larry was the only man I ever trusted and loved with all my heart. I kept the house clean, cooked, did the laundry, and ironed his uniforms. One day, he brought his socks to me and said that I ironed everything except for his socks. He was kidding, of course, but I thought he was serious about Americans wearing ironed socks. My life had finally turned a corner. For the first time I had good food, improved health, and I was happy. I wasn't living in constant fear of being beaten or cheated on.

Every week, I received at least two letters from my children. When my daughter was eight, she wrote to inform me that it had been three months since they'd heard from their father. I also received phone calls from the neighbors, telling me that my kids were playing in the street while their grandparents were working on the farm. They were not getting to school on time, and no one was helping them with their homework. The teachers were calling their father over and over, but he refused to meet with them.

I was devastated. Their grandfather had promised me that my children would be well looked after. Each time I received a letter or phone call about my kids not being looked after, tears flowed from my eyes. My darling wiped the tears from my face and promised to bring them to Germany to live with us as soon as we married. I was extremely grateful to hear him say this but was not surprised since he was such a supportive man.

Knowing his first marriage had failed, he feared that I would empty out his house and bank account while he was gone, like his previous wife. I never would have dreamed of doing such a thing. Just before Christmas, he returned from the SNCO Academy with a big surprise. It was an engagement ring! He asked me to marry him, and I couldn't tell him yes fast enough. Happiness rushed over me, and I felt as if I could fly. I had never seen a diamond or anything so shiny before. There really are no words to describe how I felt at this moment.

A few weeks after our engagement, I went to visit my children in Serbia, bringing gifts for them and their grandparents. They had never received gifts for Christmas or had a Christmas tree with decorations. Saying goodbye was much more difficult this time, but after three days, I had to return to Germany. I watched out the bus window as Jelena and Alek cried and waved goodbye. I cried all the way from Serbia to Germany, hoping that next time, I would be bringing them along.

We tried to marry in Germany, but unfortunately, foreigners wishing to marry had to wait six months for approval under German law. My husband-to-be was upset by this news and called his mother, Lois, in Cincinnati to ask what it would take for us to marry in the United States. She checked with the priest and called us back a few days later.

She told us that I needed copies of my birth certificate and divorce documents translated in English. I applied for and received a fiancée visa, and then we had all other needed documents three weeks later. Prior to leaving Germany, we purchased our wedding rings together and bought our airplane tickets.

This was my first-ever plane ride, and it was a long ten-hour nonstop flight from Frankfurt, Germany, to Cincinnati, Ohio. I was jumping with excitement but scared at the same time, digging my nails into my fiancé's arm as the plane took off. I was filled with emotion, thanking God for the plans he had made for me. I told my husband that I never dreamed of leaving my birthplace for America. He was constantly assuring me that the bad days were over and better things were coming. I held him tight and fell asleep on his shoulder. I'll never forget the day that the plane touched down onto American soil on Friday, April 8, 1994. We had to rent a car since there was no one to meet us at the airport.

Two hours later, we arrived at my fiancé's parents' house. While riding in the car, I was constantly looking out of the window amazed at everything I saw in America… Large shopping malls, fast food, cars, different churches, and houses with colored roofs. I'd never imagined such a place.

I was excited to meet his family. After a couple hours of conversation with his father, Jimmy, he told his son, "This is the right woman for you, and the one you should have married a long time ago."

His parents owned a five-bedroom house. His mom let us know that under no condition were we allowed to sleep in the same room until we were married.

We obeyed her rules. The next morning, we got up and went downtown to a restaurant for breakfast. Not having time to buy a wedding dress, my husband helped me choose a light pink blouse and a nice pink skirt at the mall in Cincinnati. On Sunday after church, we spoke with the Methodist minister about marrying us. The priest told us there was already a wedding scheduled for Saturday. Since the church would still be decorated, we could use it on Monday instead of purchasing flowers and decorations on our own.

He gave me a copy of the marriage vows to practice since my English was not perfect. I rehearsed them over and over until I got it right.

On April 11, 1994, I married the love of my life. We married in the Methodist Church where my darling grew up. The day of the wedding, it was sprinkling outside. By the time we got to the church, it was raining cats and dogs. So much rain fell that day, it seemed like the heavens had opened.

Many people told me that it was good luck to have rain on a wedding day. Rushing out of the rainstorm, I forgot my camera in the car. Since no one else had brought a camera, there were no pictures taken of the wedding. Luckily, my new father-in law caught a five-minute video. For obvious reasons, no one in my family was at the wedding, but I wish my parents and sister could have seen this moment. It was a simple ceremony, with no wedding party or reception. We didn't have the time for a reception. My new in-laws surprised us with a wedding cake at their house. I found my camera that evening and took many pictures with his family.

We left the house and checked into a hotel room that was gifted to us by his family members. We held hands and looked into each other's eyes, thanking God for letting this marriage happen. We promised to love, nurture, and take care of each other till death do us part.

My husband grew up in America while I grew up a curly-headed freckle-faced girl from a small village a world away. How did we come together? I know that only God could make this happen because "with Him, all things are possible" (Matthew 19:26). I will never forget that day for as long as I live.

Soon after we married, we flew to Salt Lake City, Utah, where my husband had to work for a week. We told the stewardess that we had just married. They flew us first class with a bottle of champagne. Once his work was over, every day we had plans to drive and visit different places and enjoying each other's company.

We had a chance to visit the Salt Lake and the Teton Mountains in Wyoming. For the first time, I saw dinosaur bones in a museum and learned about American Indian history. Another day, we drove two hundred miles to an Indian Reservation but encountered hundreds of free-range cows running toward our car. My husband took action by turning the car around. I couldn't believe the things I was now getting to experience right before my eyes.

Eventually, we flew back to Germany. My darling had to get back to work, and I had to check on my kids. As a new military wife, I went to get my military ID card so I could shop on base. We began shopping for bedroom furniture for the kids and began planning how we would bring them from Serbia.

We moved to a bigger house so they could have their own rooms. I also began the process of looking for a school for my children. I called my children to let them know of the marriage and that the next time I visited, I would be bringing them home with me.

Two weeks later, a neighbor called. Alexandar was riding his bicycle in the street when he was hit by a car. My heart stopped. It threw him into the bushes, which broke his landing. His grandfather immediately took Alek to the emergency room. X-rays revealed that he had no broken bones, just some bruises and scrapes. This was an immense relief. I knew God was protecting my son, but I wanted him in my sight for once and for all.

CHAPTER 19

Back to Serbia

I was terrified every time I watched the news. After Yugoslavian President Tito died in 1980, a situation arose between six states: Slovenia and Croatia were the first states to declare independence, then Bosnia and Herzegovina, followed by Macedonia and Montenegro. Situation heated up between six states because they all declared their independence from Yugoslavia. However, this independence did not happen without fighting and ethnic cleansing between religions. States started to remove citizens from these areas. Land owners became angry and did not want to give up their lifelong properties. People started killing each other to protect their belongings.

Politicians and fake media fueled the fire and started to spread lies and blame all this conflict on Serbian people through all broadcasting resources. War between religions made the situation worse when Serbian Orthodox churches were destroyed. Anger between citizens of Yugoslavia caused outrageous human casualty numbers because of the fighting. The North Atlantic Treaty Organization (NATO) got involved and brought in troops on the ground and in the air to help keep the peace.

Bombs fell on Serbia for seventy-two days. I cried, praying to God that someone would put an end to the war. I lived in fear that one day, I would receive a phone call notifying me of a terrible tragedy to my family members. I spoke with other relatives in Serbia. They informed me about planes missing their targets, bombed hospitals, hitting buses and trains that burned people alive. NATO forces bombed radio stations, roads, and bridges, and cut off communication to the city.

I had to communicate with my sister in Austria many times to find out what was going on. Travel between Serbia and Germany was very complicated because of the restrictions and refugees. I had to plan a route that I could use to retrieve my children from a hostile area. It was a complicated process to get their visas to leave Serbia for Germany.

The media coverage was emotionally draining, and all I could do was pray. I stood strong with my God, knowing to "not be afraid of them; the LORD your God himself will fight for you" (Deuteronomy 3:22).

I called my children to tell them I was coming for them. They rejoiced when they got the news.

On June 20, 1994, I sat on a bus in Mannheim, Germany. The conflict had settled down, and they were out for summer break. I traveled throughout the night and changed buses at the Serbian border since German buses weren't allowed in Serbia or vice versa. The weather was sweltering. I arrived in Belgrade at a bus station that was engulfed in a cloud of cigarette smoke and crowds of sweating people.

I went to collect my luggage from beneath the bus among a rush of people and felt someone open my purse to take my wallet. I shouted, stopping him, and turned to him face-to-face with his beady, dark eyes. I let him know that he would not prowl on innocent people for his own sake. He tried to distract me and offer help with my luggage, but I refused. I was on a mission to take my kids back, and nothing was going to stop me. Once again God stepped in and put a stop to evil.

My two beautiful children were waiting with their grandmother when I arrived. I hugged them for what felt like forever. I was so happy to have my children in my arms and smell their sweet skin. I thanked their grandmother for watching after them and hugged her as well.

I told them that this time, they were leaving and would be with me for good. Since they were finishing school, this was the best time to apply for their visas. I stayed with their grandparents until I had all the necessary documentation.

Early in the morning, I rode a bus and arrived at the German consulate at 5:00 a.m., only to see a mile-long line. I contemplated whether I should stand in the long, hot line or come back. I decided to stay and waited my turn. I went every day for three weeks to stand in line. On the days I got in to see somebody, they either wanted new documentation, didn't recognize my information, or needed another step completed.

When I finally got to the office, they informed me that they did not accept US military ID cards as a form of iden-tification. I would need to get a visa. They wanted a letter from my husband as well, indicating that he was expecting me back in Germany. In addition to all this documentation, they required a letter from my children's father allowing me to take the kids out of Serbia. I had not figured out yet how I would convince their father to sign off. I began feeling hopeless again, not knowing how long it would take to track him down.

I was filled with trepidation at the idea of seeing my ex-husband again. I had to do it to get the papers signed. There was no way around it, and I kept telling myself, "It's for my kids' sake."

We met at his parents' house on neutral ground. There was no handshake or hug or friendly atmosphere or conversation. When he entered the room, he pulled a shiny, metallic gun from his waistband and dropped it on the table as a way of intimidation, like a cowboy in a Western would do, while asking, "What do you want from me?" He had a lit cigarette between his fingers in the other hand, and he was sharply dressed.

I told him, "I did not come to fight with you." I explained to him nicely what the consulate needed me to do to take our kids to Germany for the summer. I need their father's signature to get the kids' visas.

He told me that he would not sign the documents.

I persuaded him that they would only be spending the summer with me. He cared nothing about our children, except that they were a bargaining chip to use in an attempt to make my life miserable one more time. I told him that they were becoming a handful for his parents, and it was not their responsibility to constantly take care of our kids.

He took a big puff on his cigarette and exhaled smoke in my face as his last act. I replied, "Look, I did not come all this way to get revenge. I have more important things to do," I said.

He finally signed the documents after endless questions, and I thanked him. He ordered me to bring them back once the summer was over. I promised… Little did he know.

He asked many personal questions about my new husband and marriage. I didn't feel the need to answer him. I did, however, have to brag about the wonderful man that my husband was and how he would provide a good life for our kids. He picked up his gun and walked out of the room. No goodbyes from either of us. I thanked God that he was by my side and protected me in this situation.

The day after he signed the papers, I went to my church to light a candle, gave the priest money for the church, and prayed for a safe and smooth transition back to Germany. This church was where my happiness and miracles began. It was such a special church to me.

Now I had to get those visas. I went to the consulate at 3:00 p.m., but due to the long line, I had to come back the second day. For days, I stood in the line from 5:00 a.m. to 3:00 p.m. with little food or water. I lost twelve pounds, waiting in the hot sun.

One hot and sunny day, my nephew, Zoran, came to visit me in front of the embassy. He brought me a sandwich, water, and an old, rusty, blue beach chair (kid's size) to sit under the shade and eat. I was scared to eat because I didn't want to leave the line to use the restroom. Even as the hot rays of the sun beat down on my scalp, I refused to get out of line. I placed the documents above me to shield the heat and protect my head from sunburn.

My nephew helped me to not lose my place in line. I was so thankful for him doing this for me. Everyone was trying to escape the madness of the war. They all wanted out of the country. The guards of the consulate manipulated these poor refugees, promising to get them inside by pocketing their money. I feel gullible one desperate day, almost offering money to the guards. Thankfully, my nephew Zoran disclosed what was being done.

While waiting in line the second day, I observed an argument between the guards and people who paid the bribe money the day before. The guards took their money but refused to let them in.

I was determined not to leave Serbia without my children. I contacted my husband in Germany and told him that I could not make it back. I was almost out of money, energy, and patience. My husband contacted the German police and American consulate to tell them that his wife and her two children were stuck in Serbia. The German police sent a fax called a *familijen-cuzamen-firung*, giving the details needed by the German consulate to get three emergency visas to put the family together.

Three weeks later, on the Fourth of July holiday in Serbia, most people assumed the consulate would be closed. There were only three people in line. I was finally able to enter the consulate office and finish the visa applications. The lady told me that she had received the fax paperwork from Germany, and the visas would be ready in two days. It was the best news I'd heard in a long time.

After they received the less-than-congenial demand from the German police, things moved along very quickly...that is, until we hit another wall. The German consulate notified me that we needed three visas to get through Austria due to the ongoing border conflict. Now I had to get three visas to travel through Austria, where we were required to have them just to cross the border. Border agents were afraid that we would be part of the influx of refugees without proper visas trying to flee the war in Serbia.

I went to see my half-sister Vera and told her of my dilemma. She told me if I wanted to get visas the same day, I would need to be in front of the Austrian consulate at 7:00 p.m. the night before. She promised me that she would go with me.

At 7:00 p.m., we were the first ones in line. Fifteen minutes later, twenty more people arrived. By 10:00 p.m., the line swelled to over a hundred. We leaned against each other during the night, talking until we ran out of stories and fell asleep. One of the interesting stories she told me that night I will never forget. My half-sister told me when she was fourteen years old, she went to live with biological mother Djurka. She so eagerly wanted to live with her mother. However, her wishes did not come true. She only stayed for a very short time because her mother had five other siblings to take care of. Her mother constantly threatened to sell her to the Turks. She was terrified, ran away, and came back to live with my father. The threats ended her relationship forever with her mother. Both of us was mentally exhausted, and we slept on the concrete steps, and thank God, we were blessed with good weather and protected.

By 5:30 a.m., the throng of people was innumerable. The consulate doors opened at 8:00 a.m. I told my sister to go home because she had to go to work. She needed the rest and was very tired. I hugged her and thanked her.

When I got into the consulate, I did not realize so much paperwork needed to be filled out. I did not understand all the paperwork, but a gentleman at the front desk was available to help fill out the documents for a few dinars. He helped me fill out the paperwork and turned it in for me, telling me to come back at 3:00 p.m. to pick up my visas.

The area around the Austrian consulate was located by a beautiful park with wooden benches under shady trees. I felt relief in the fresh air, listening to the birds sing, knowing that soon, I'd have my kids in Germany. I encouraged myself that it was almost over and thanked God for carrying me this far.

I napped on a stiff bench for several hours, then went to get something to eat. I was afraid of oversleeping and missing my appointment. After I got the visas, the feelings were of extreme relief. When I walked out of the Austrian embassy with the visas on July 11, 1994, I was wide awake, full of determination, and I went straight to the bus station to find out how to get us all back to Germany as soon as possible. I caught a break, thanks to my nephew stopping me from paying a bribe to those patrols. I immediately purchased three tickets for July 13. I had the tickets in hand two days later.

I went to my former in-laws' home to give my kids the exciting news: we would be leaving Serbia for good and to start packing. The kids were brimming with excitement and began shoving clothes into their plastic bags. I told them not to take too much since we could get new clothes in Germany. I told them how good God had been to us throughout this entire ordeal and that He had heard my prayers. I thanked their grandparents for taking care of them. Their grandpa wished them the best and wanted to stay in contact with them. Their grandparents packed us fresh bread, smoked ham, and water to have on the trip, which was a blessing. He joked with Alek, "Eat all the ham. Germany doesn't have that kind of cooking."

I ran to my neighbor's house to borrow their phone to call my husband and tell him that God has lifted us and we would be leaving soon. My husband's intervention made this all happen, or we would be stuck in Serbia for a long time. He was relieved to hear from me and told me he would be waiting impatiently for us in Mannheim. I paid my neighbors for the phone call and ran back to my kids.

After a long and exhausting three weeks, my children and I left Belgrade bus station forever at 3:30 p.m. Before we left, Vera and her family came to say goodbye. She cried happy tears as we left. My ex-husband and his girlfriend came to bid the kids farewell, fully expecting that I would bring them back to Serbia at the end of the summer.

July 13 was the happiest day of my life, after the day I married my darling. My two children were by my side, and I thanked God for seeing us through.

As we left the bus station, passengers waved to their family members. We were traveling on a bus full of chain-smokers. The carpet stank of smoke and body odor. We traveled for eight hours. All three of us got off somewhere behind the Hungarian border at 11:30 p.m. to wait for another bus.

The bus dropped us off in the middle of nowhere. There was no sign of life or a sound to be heard. No buildings or bus station, or any other people. Just dark country roads. It looked like somebody's farm. My mind went through the possibilities of what might become of us if the bus never showed up. We were the only three at the bus stop, with only darkness surrounding us. My kids were terrified, so for their sake, I suppressed my own fears. I reassured them that God would take care of us, and we prayed together.

Finally, after an hour of waiting, the bus arrived. My relief was short-lived, however. Even after people got off the bus, it was still so full we had to stand. The bus driver told us for safety reasons he couldn't take us since the bus was already overloaded. I begged him not to leave me in the middle of nowhere with two small children. We would sit on the floor, anywhere to avoid staying in this dark, isolated place. He still refused.

Panic set in until one of the passengers spoke up. He said to the driver, "You will not leave her and those two kids in this darkness." He offered his seat to us so that we weren't left on the side of the road. I thanked this man profusely and blessed him for his kindness.

The bus driver just shrugged his shoulders and said, "I will take them as long as you agree to give up your seat and stand." The gentleman patted my son Alek on his head and assured him that he would not be left behind in the dark. Here again, God performed a miracle in the middle of the night.

CHAPTER 20

Adjusting to Life in Germany

We boarded the bus, tied our bags under the seat, and my kids' faces went from sad to happy. We traveled all through the night while the children slept on my lap. By the time the bus had arrived, my legs were numb, and we had eaten all the food provided by the grandparents, wishing we had more. We finally arrived in Mannheim at 9:00 a.m. on July 14, 1994.

My husband was waiting for us, anxious to meet my children for the first time. I know he was happy to see me, but at the same time, he was probably wondering what he'd gotten himself into. My darling Larry met the kids and asked how the trip had been. My heart could've exploded in that moment. He hugged each of us tightly and told me how much he'd missed me. I had missed those strong arms around me.

When we got home, I introduced my kids to their very own rooms and indoor bathroom, both a first for them. Our home was clean and beautiful; the food was so much better than my kids had ever dreamed of.

It was hard for my husband and children to communicate because of the language barrier. The kids began learning English right away with me. We signed Alek up to play soccer for a German team. This helped him learn both languages and make friends at the same time.

At first, everything was exciting and shiny, but after the new wore off, Alek expressed he missed home. He didn't like the fact that we had rules, whereas his grandparents did not. They were allowed to stay awake as late as they liked to. This expression of wanting to return home resulted in Alek spending time in his room as punishment.

Nothing was easy for my husband, either. It was a challenging adjustment with a nine- and ten-year-old. My husband enrolled Jelena in the sixth grade and Alek in fifth grade in an American school, Kaiserslautern, in Germany. Three months after the kids started school, they had English down pat.

Because of the time difference between the countries, Alek had a hard time staying awake and concentrating after 1:00 p.m. He was used to being done with class and ready for his nap by then. He would lay on the carpet floor and tell the teacher he was done studying for the day. We were called to the school by his English teacher, Mr. Gross, to solve this problem. The teacher and Alek became good friends.

Both kids became good students and received good grades and awards. My darling would help them with their homework until late at night. He loved them and called them his own. He never referred to them as his "stepchildren." Soon after, they began calling him their dad. Our lives were changing as we became a happy family—loving each other, supporting each other, and praying together. God always heard our prayers and surrounded us with happiness.

I adored my husband. For the first time, I celebrated Christmas as a family with my new love and children by my side. They finally had a real Christmas tree with gifts beneath it. He was the first person to buy me a Christmas present, ever.

The children progressed in school, and Alek continued to play soccer, with his new dad supporting him at games. The kids called their grandparents in Serbia to tell them how much things had improved.

The kids became much disciplined, but it wasn't easy. Thankfully, I had the help of my husband in raising them. They made their beds before school each morning. Even from a young age, Jelena was always very organized and particular. She would never let me clean her room and insisted on doing it exactly the way she wanted. Her clothes were well organized, as was her desk and bathroom. Jelena would spend many hours in her room practicing different hairstyles and makeup. She had no idea at the time that this was going to be her future job.

Both kids were good listeners and obeyed our rules. Two years after the children arrived in Germany, I called and reached out to their father in requesting financial support until I could get a job, but he refused. Although he was a successful businessman, he had no interest in supporting them. He told me that he wouldn't help me, and I was on my own. It broke my heart that he cared so little for his own children. Both God and my darling supported us, and I'm thankful to them both.

Over the next four years, my children returned to Serbia once. It was the first time they'd flown on an airplane alone. I don't know who was more frightened, them or me. They expressed a desire to visit their grandparents, but they wanted nothing to do with their father. Contact between them and their biological father dwindled down to nothing. He never supported them financially or remembered them on their birthdays or Christmas. He had two children with the girlfriend whom he never married. He borrowed money from the bank to open his own business and lived a life of luxury, while ignoring them completely.

My children told me heartbreaking stories of how they were not welcome in their biological father's new apartment. He dropped them off at the gates of the house of his parents, telling his father to deal with them because they were a huge embarrassment to him. When he did decide to spend time with them, he physically and verbally abused them. A year later, he lost his business, was forced to declare bankruptcy, and his girlfriend walked out on him…just as he had walked out on me, taking their children with her. He thought the young beauty queen would be his forever woman, but karma thought otherwise. He currently lives alone with his mother and had no part in raising any of his children.

God wants us to forgive. Colossians 3:13 tells us to "put up with each other, and forgive anyone who does you wrong, just as Christ has forgiven you." I struggled to forgive him after all the times he had hurt me. After some time, I did forgive him, and I still pray for him to this day.

Even when I felt like I was suffering alone, God was always with me, helping along the way. He walked with me throughout my life, protected me in the worst situations, and gave me a future I never dreamed of. He took care of my children when we were apart and kept them safe in all circumstances.

> Neither height nor depth, nor anything else in all creation, will be able to separate us from the love of God that is in Christ Jesus our LORD.
> —Romans 8:39

CHAPTER 21

USA

In July of 1998, my husband made the decision to retire from the Air Force after twenty-six years of service. If he continued to serve, he would have had to relocate for one year to Korea for a remote assignment and send us alone to the United States. Instead, we headed to America as a family.

The kids and I had to apply for visas and green cards. We also needed a battery of medical tests, along with shot records, which turned out to be quite expensive. Since I didn't have the kids' records, their grandfather sent them to us. Without their grandfather's help, we would have come to a stopping point.

I could not get my medical records because I found out from my half-brother that all records were burned and destroyed in the war. There was no way to track down anyone in Kosovo. Everyone I knew from Kosovo had fled. I was required to get my shots all over again. My arm was swollen and sore for a week. I wish I had gotten my shot records at the same time I got my birth certificate in 1991, the last time I visited Kosovo.

The military packed up our belongings, and the kids said goodbye to their friends. On August 24, 1998, we left Germany for the United States and landed in Cincinnati, Ohio. This was my kids' first airplane ride to America. We stayed with my in-laws through November 1998. We all struggled during this adjustment. We all missed German food and friends, but most importantly, my husband missed his German beer. Getting the kids enrolled in school, learning how to drive, and finding a job was a task. Learning to drive at the age of thirty-eight was not easy. In Germany, they had mass transit to get you to your destination, unlike in Cincinnati. My husband hired a driving instructor to make it a little easier on me. I had difficulty understanding the questions on the computer-based test. I studied day and night to pass the driver's exam. My husband was busy developing his résumé and applied for many jobs but had no luck. Two months later, he received a call from Robins Air Force Base in Warner Robins, Georgia. They hired him on the spot, without an interview, because of his good references from his former boss in Germany. Just like that, the job was his!

We began house hunting. I fell in love with the small city. We found a house and made an offer. We left early in the morning on November 13, 1998, for Georgia. We thanked the in-laws for letting us stay with them, but we were glad to be moving south. I did not enjoy my time in Cincinnati. Everything was spread out: shopping malls, grocery stores, gas stations. It was such a big city, with cold weather almost year-round. We all wanted to find a place that was not as cold as Germany. When we arrived in Warner Robins, the house was not quite ready, so we briefly lived in a two-bedroom apartment.

I stayed very busy the first few months of living in Georgia. We enrolled the children in Houston County High School. My son began playing soccer again. I finally got my green card. I passed my driver's test and got a license. We moved into our new house a week before Christmas. Everything was working out for the better.

Our furniture arrived from Germany a couple days before Christmas. I was excited to arrange and decorate the new house, making it a home. Our neighbors even brought us welcoming pies with their Southern hospitality. I had never experienced such friendly people.

The next spring, I got my first full-time job at a new McDonald's. I was very excited to be providing money to help pay the bills. I made $5.40 an hour, which increased every six months from being a good, hardworking employee. Mr. Cliff, the owner, always requested that I made his breakfast or lunch when he came to visit his employees. He always complimented me on my cleanliness and wished he had more employees like me. These kind words gave me more energy and made me work harder. My husband and I soon purchased my first car.

My next goal was to become a US citizen. In order to apply, we had to live in the United States for three years. My kids and I had to study American history and pass a one-hundred-question test, recite the Pledge of Allegiance, and be able to write in English. The applications were expensive, but we wanted to do things right.

Nine months after applying, a call came from Atlanta telling us that it was time to take the test. We all took no time to get there. We woke up early, and I had nervous butterflies the entire drive to Atlanta. I sat down to take the test, prepared for anything. The instructor asked who was the first president, what do the stars and stripes on the flag represent, and why is Fourth of July celebrated. I breathed a huge sigh of relief. I finished the test and exited, waiting patiently for the news... We passed!

We had a swearing-in ceremony on the same day where I pledged to the flag of the United States of America. As I walked out of the building, I lifted my hands to God, thanking him. In 2001, we became American citizens. We celebrated with a big party in our home, inviting all our friends and neighbors. My son's soccer team even brought a huge cake, saying "Congratulations on American Citizenship."

We are so thankful to live in a country so full of opportunity to make the best of ourselves. After two and a half years at McDonald's and never being late to work, I left, disillusioned with the younger employees' lack of work ethic. I took a job with a better paycheck and benefits at Kroger Supermarket. I started out as a cashier but had difficulties with the language barrier, so I bagged groceries instead. While working at Kroger, I met a frequent friendly customer named Mary. She only wanted me to bag her groceries because I was so organized and did a great job and always wore a smile when she checked out. Her kindness was a blessing to me, and I will always be grateful that the Lord gave me a friend like her. After six months of constantly urging me toward a new position, I left Kroger to work with Mary. That was one of my best decisions.

After three and a half years at Kroger, I began working for the Cantrell Center for Physical Therapy and Wellness on January 3, 2005. I have now been working there for over fifteen happy years as head of housekeeping.

Just as soon as things were going well, we got a sucker punch. At sixteen years old, Alek came home from school, feeling sick with a high fever. My husband was away on business for a week, so I was alone. His fever continued to soar, so I took him to the doctor. The doctor did a blood test and gave him a muscle relaxer shot for the pain. The blood test showed no infection, so we went home.

I called the doctor again because Alek got no relief as the night progressed. He recommended a different medication, but it failed to work, and soon Alek couldn't even stand up. On the fifth day of his agony, my husband returned home, and we took Alek to the hospital. We found out through testing that the pain he was going through was his ruptured appendix that needed to be removed immediately. The doctor was surprised since his blood test showed no signs. They tried to remove it through minimally invasive surgery but ended up having to do more extensive surgery to clean out the infection. His surgery lasted two grueling hours.

The doctor told my son that he was lucky to be in such good physical condition from years of playing soccer. If not, he would not have survived. Alek had to stay in the hospital for a week in the intensive care unit. When we saw him after the surgery, he was as white as the sheet that covered him.

My heart dropped, and so did I to the floor. I thought that he was gone. My darling picked me up, reassuring me that the surgery was successful, and he was only pale. Fear gripped me, and I began to have an anxiety attack. My husband and I took turns staying the night on a thin cot with a clumpy pillow at the hospital. A week later, the infection was gone, and he was released to go home. He had lost so much weight; he was all skin and bones. It took three months for him to fully recover. Once he was feeling better, he was right back on the soccer field. I thank God for saving my son. Again, that was truly a big miracle received from God after Alek survived five days with a ruptured appendix.

After things returned to normal and everyone was in good health, we took a family vacation to Destin, Florida. We were excited to spend our family vacation on the beach. With little experience of the beach, we were not prepared and became severely sunburned on the first day. We all laid on the cold tile in the kitchen floor, smothered in aloe vera. Nobody wanted to talk or be touched because of the pain and blisters.

My husband and I decided the next vacation would be to the mountains in North Carolina. We loved it so much, we visited three times a year. We took long weekends to walk the mountains, relax by the river, grill out, read books, and have a good time.

When Alek turned eighteen, he attended college on a soccer scholarship. He had such a great relationship with the players, coaches, and even the trainer who paid him to mow the grass on the soccer field.

Alek called to inform us of what happened one sunny day after coming back from mowing. He arrived at his dorm room that he shared with two other friends, and he took the trash out. He had left the door open, and as he returned to his room, he noticed two armed robbers threatening him to hand over his wallet. He tried to back out of his room, hoping that one of his roommates would see the situation. With his roommates busy in their own rooms, they were no help. He silently prayed, afraid that he would be killed and never see his family again.

He was overcome with peace while looking at the icon of Christ hanging from his wall. He glanced at the icon and asked God for help. God saved his life, but the robbers got away with his wallet and ran off with his identification cards. As it turned out, he only had a couple of dollars, his driver's license, and student ID card in his wallet. My son reported the incident to the police. Unfortunately, his wallet was never recovered, and the robbers were never found.

Shortly after this incident, God once again intervened and saved Alek in an automobile accident. It was a dreary, rainy day with wet road conditions. As he was driving downtown after school, he began to stop, but the wet conditions caused his brakes to lock up, and he slid into the intersection, impacting the side of a SUV. His car was totaled, but thank God, there were no injuries to my son or to the other driver.

CHAPTER 22

Heartaches

On one of our trips to the North Carolina Mountains, my husband began complaining of difficulty breathing, with sharp pains in his chest and shoulders. My worry increased as we climbed higher in altitude since cell phone reception was spotty to nonexistent in the mountains. I recommended that we head home immediately and for him to see a doctor on the way into North Carolina, but he refused.

I kept encouraging him that once we got back home, he should see the doctor. I worried because he was overweight, had a sedentary, rather stressful job, and exercised very little, preferring to sit down as soon as he came home from work. He refused to see the doctor. I began to pressure him to make a doctor's appointment, even offering to make the appointment for him myself. He still refused. He told me that he was a grown man and that if he needed to see a doctor, he would make the appointment.

A week after coming back from vacation, he finally called me at work to tell me he had made an appointment for himself. His cardiologist performed a nuclear stress test, which he failed. The doctor then ordered a catheterization. I drove him to the hospital, and he was admitted over the weekend. The catheterization took place that following Monday. I hugged him and wished him good luck. He was fearless as we watched him being rolled through the door to the operating room.

Jelena and I anxiously waited for the results in a cold waiting room. We held each other's hands, fighting tears. About an hour later, a nurse appeared to take us into his room. The doctor told us that the test found three blockages in the arteries around his heart. One was 95 percent blocked, and the other two arteries were 75 and 60 percent blocked, respectively. Jelena and I looked at each other, then looked at my husband. We were devastated. Since his cardiologist did not have the necessary experience to insert the stents, he was transported by ambulance the same night to the Macon Heart Institute, where we waited for the surgery to be completed.

We prayed during the entire surgery. Shortly after the procedure, he told us he was feeling better already. His breathing and energy had improved. The doctor warned him and me that if he were to have a heart attack and survived, he would require open-heart surgery. It was a wake-up call for him to start exercising and eat healthier. He needed to change his lifestyle and eating habits.

Two weeks later, we hired a personal trainer in the Cantrell Center. He started losing weight, watching his diet, and began feeling better. Unfortunately, after three months, he lapsed back into his old habits. He quit exercising, began eating out with his coworkers every day, and consumed a high amount of fat and sugar. As soon as he came home from work, he would immediately fall asleep in his king chair.

Six months after his last hospital visit, he was walking from a meeting with his coworkers to his office. He was unable to keep up with them, and one of his coworkers noticed he was pale and weak. Knowing his health condition, they began to worry. Larry told them he was going to sit on a bench and rest but for them to go on. They knew about his conditions and put him in the car and drove him to the hospital.

My husband forbade them to contact me. One of his coworkers walked out of the emergency room and called me anyways. I immediately informed my boss of the situation, left work, and headed straight for the hospital.

My husband was really surprised when he saw me, crossing his arms over his chest, questioning, "What are you doing here?" with a smile on his face. He acted if nothing was wrong.

I replied, "What are *you* doing here?"

After another catheterization was done, the doctor found that some artery plaque went through the stents and blocked his artery. Once again, the ambulance transported him to the Heart Institute of Macon, where the cardiovascular surgeon inserted larger stents plus two others, a total of four stents. Following this procedure, my husband had to stay overnight in the hospital, and the doctor gave him medicine to help clear the plaque from his arteries. I stayed by his side through it all and didn't leave him.

My husband did not seem to realize how serious his condition was. God was giving him a chance to turn things around. I tried to remind him that his diet needed to change. On top of his blockages, he was also diabetic and hypertensive.

I myself began to have problems with high blood pressure. On January 2, 2015, I was hospitalized when my blood pressure reading reached 227/117 mmHg. My heart was racing at one hundred beats per minute, my left arm tingled, and my lips were numb. I was cold and shivering, and after fifteen minutes of this, my husband called 911.

During my two-day hospital stay, the doctors performed numerous tests and found that I had a 50 percent blockage in my left kidney and a 50 percent blockage in my carotid arteries.

In March of 2016, Larry was unable to finish his dinner, complaining of heartburn. He checked his blood pressure, and it didn't look too good. He proceeded to take his medication, Norvasc. Not long after, he had an appointment for another catheterization, which showed a 100 percent blockage in his artery. Since the artery had grown inside the muscle of his heart, nothing could be done other than to prescribe a different blood thinner.

Two weeks after beginning the new blood thinner, his feet began to swell. I forced him to go see the cardiologist about it. He went to the doctor and was told not to worry about it, as long as his blood pressure improved. He went back home and hoped the swelling would go down.

On April 11, 2016, we celebrated our twenty-second wedding anniversary. During dinner, he told me that his best decision in his life was to marry me. He loved me and held my hands. He gave me a gift, a Fitbit to help track my health. Little did I know that this would be our last anniversary dinner.

The night of April 14, 2016 at 2:00 a.m., I began to feel sick. I was dizzy, had a severe headache, and my chest was burning. I became nauseated and came to the point where I was unable to breathe. My husband rushed me to the emergency room, telling me he'd never seen me so sick in our twenty-four years together.

In front of the hospital, I tried to take a deep breath and fell to my knees at the front of the emergency room door. I told the nurse I was having the symptoms of a heart attack. They quickly took care of me. A blood test showed that everything was okay physically, but I had been taking the wrong combination of medication. My doctor had me on an anxiety pill, heartburn medication, and two blood-pressure pills. God spared me that night. I was released on Sunday morning. I left the hospital and went straight to church to thank God.

On April 21, 2016, I left for work at the usual time, 5:00 a.m. Before leaving, my husband looked at me with sleepy eyes and told me that he checked on me twice during the night and reminded me that we were taking our granddaughter, Jasmine, to soccer practice when I returned home. I gently kissed his warm cheek, told him I loved him, then left for work.

I called him at 9:00 a.m. on his cell phone, but there was no answer. I left him a message, asking him to call me back. I assumed that he was in a meeting and didn't want to be interrupted during those times. I figured I would speak with him when I got home. I finished work at 1:30 p.m. and stayed to exercise until 3:00 p.m.

When I arrived at home, I noticed his car was still in the front of the house, and the trash can was not at the curb. I thought he must not have been feeling well and stayed home from work. As I walked into the house and called for him, there was no answer. I walked into our bedroom, and the bed was still unmade. I had an unsettling feeling.

I set my purse on the floor next to the dining room table and looked up to see him slumped against the wall on the kitchen floor, his glasses knocked askew on the top of his head as he had fallen. I began screaming and hoped that what I thought had happened had not. I thought that he may have just passed out. I tried to move him and found him unresponsive. His body lay there, cold and hard. I was in a state of shock. My love of twenty-four years was gone.

I ran outside and called 911. The 911 dispatcher told me to stop screaming and crying because she couldn't understand me. She tried calming me down and asked if I could give him CPR. It was too late. He was already cold. The dispatcher told me she would send the ambulance to my house. I sobbed so loudly on the concrete driveway in front of the garage, pounding the concrete with my fist, the whole neighborhood had to have known what just happened.

I poured my pain and anger out to God. Why did He not help my husband when he was alone and needed Him the most? Had I not struggled enough? Why had God taken the love of my life at only sixty-two years of age? I was not ready to live without him. We had plans to enjoy his retirement, only two years away. We dreamed of all the places we would explore together.

Now I had to start a new life without him and felt nothing but despair. Even with all my struggles in Serbia, this was by far the worst.

I called my children and friends at work. Everyone quickly showed up to support me. I'll never forget the tragic moment of shaking him, begging him to wake up and screaming out to God. After twenty-four years together, I had to say goodbye to the love of my life and best friend, a wonderful father and grandfather. Watching the ambulance take him away, I felt a piece of me leaving as well. My heart was broken into innumerable pieces.

We are still grieving to this day, four years later. Losing someone so beloved is physically, emotionally, and spiritually exhausting. Even writing this, the pain pierces my heart like a jagged sword.

My husband was buried with military honors. During the funeral, many people told me they would be there for me and help with anything I needed. But they were hollow words. After the funeral, most disappeared back into their lives as I tried piecing mine together.

When I gathered the strength and energy, I began to take care of my home again. As I was sweeping the kitchen floor, I found an aspirin in the corner where my husband fell. I think he had chest pain, tried taking it, but never had the chance. If only he had reached for the phone, instead of medicine. The emergency responders and his cardiologist stated that he had a heart attack.

Other than my children, I didn't hear from many people. I stayed with my daughter for three months. I would come back to the house during the day and leave at nighttime. I couldn't stand to be in the empty house alone, certainly not at night. I lost twenty-two pounds during this time. I had no appetite.

I began to attend a grief support class. I had to learn how to fix meals for one, watch our favorite shows alone, sleep alone, pay the bills, and become the sole decision-maker. When I went to the grocery store, I would aimlessly walk around and leave the store with empty hands. So many times, I would eat a sandwich in the car alone because I could not eat in the house of memories that we built together.

The new responsibilities were overwhelming. I'm forever thankful to my coworkers. They were so supportive, and my dear friends cried with me.

I began visiting his gravesite three times a week, but the more I visited, the more I had panic attacks and heart troubles. I begged God to tell my darling husband how lost I felt without him. I know that one day we will be reunited, but if I could only embrace him and talk to him one more time. His children and grandchildren miss him terribly.

The grandchildren kept asking when Papa would be coming back. Would he be there for their birthdays? For Christmas? I kept telling them that Papa was in heaven with God.

"How far is heaven?" they asked. "Why can't we visit him?"

They wrote letters for me to give him when I went to visit the cemetery. Our youngest granddaughter, Adrijanna, asked me for Papa's phone number so she could call him. They didn't want any Christmas gifts—just for Papa to come home. My second granddaughter, Isabel, asked me to please dig Papa up and bring him home. They missed him so much. To all three of the girls, Papa was their hero. Jasmine, the oldest, will always remember him coming to cheer her on at her soccer games and celebrating a win at Chick-fil-A afterward.

CHAPTER 23

A New Beginning

At my next visit to our cardiologist, he asked about my husband. I was surprised that he would ask me that question. I thought, *Why is he asking me what happened to my husband? My opinion? He prescribed him too many blood thinner medications.*

After I told him what happened, he explained that as a result of the blockages in his heart, one of the arteries exploded, and he lost consciousness. His heart was fighting for blood, and he wouldn't have lived longer than forty seconds. The doctor told me he didn't suffer because everything happened so fast. His cold, unsympathetic words did nothing to ease my pain of losing my best friend.

Over the next seven months, I went to the emergency room six different times for hypertension. I had not been able to sleep at night with my blood pressure so high. In June, the electrophysiologist performed an ablation on my heart at the Macon Heart Institute.

This did nothing for my heart problems, so I decided to get a second opinion at a better hospital. I insisted that my primary physician refer me to the Mayo Clinic in Jacksonville, Florida, where I found a wonderful cardiologist. I didn't understand my high blood pressure since I exercised daily and watched what I ate. After two and a half years of struggling with high blood pressure, the cardiologist prescribed a different medication. He told me to quit taking my three old prescriptions and began taking one new medicine. In just two days, my blood pressure problem was alleviated. My heart slowed down, and my life was back to normal. God sent me this perfect cardiologist.

I continued going to church every Sunday and prayed even more earnestly than before for his forgiveness of my anger toward him. I knew I would need God's help to get through this. For about a year before his passing, I began to have a recurring nightmare. In retrospect, I realize God wanted to show me something, although I had no idea at the time. In the nightmare, I would see a storm rip through my house. Strong winds blew through shattering glass. Water flooded the inside of the house and walls were falling apart. The rain fell so hard that the house collapsed. Every time I had this nightmare, it was so real and painful to see my house gone with nothing left behind. I was standing behind what was left of my home and watching the water take it all away. I always questioned why I had this same nightmare every night for one year.

I felt this nightmare come true, as my home turned into a house without my darling in it. After he passed, I never had the dream again.

CHAPTER 24

Dreams

Every day, I habitually prayed in the same spot where my husband took his last breath on the kitchen floor. Not having my husband or anyone to talk to, I leaned heavily on God. I read my Bible and lit my candle. This is the only place where I felt safe. I continued to deal with my own health problems on top of the fresh anxiety of losing my beloved. A few times, Father John, our parish priest, prayed for me and anointed me with holy oil and holy water. This brought me a great deal of comfort.

I asked God to send my husband in a dream to tell me what happened on that unforgettable day. After many nights of praying, God finally granted me this. The dream was so real. In the dream, we were sleeping soundly in the comfort of each other's presence when he suddenly jumped out of bed and scrambled for his blood-pressure medication. He yelled out, "Oh my god! My blood pressure is so high!"

I ran to him, dialing 911. He began walking but became disoriented. Instead of walking into the kitchen, he ended up walking into my closet. I told him to go into the kitchen, which he finally managed. I stood beside him when he entered the kitchen, and the dream abruptly ended. I believe God put a wall between us so I could not enter the kitchen. I was not prepared to see what happened next.

Every day, my mind would always go back to the same question. Could any of his nine medications that he had taken daily have killed him? I wanted him to return to my dreams to tell me what had happened.

In January 2017, this wish came true. In my dream, I was standing in the laundry room, folding my clothes with my mind occupied. I heard footsteps walking down the hall toward the laundry room. I was frightened because nobody else was home. The alarm system was on, and I knew I should be safe. I peeped out of the door a couple times, but still no one appeared.

Suddenly, my darling was standing at the door. He was wearing his brown pants, blue jacket, and tennis shoes. Before he could get his words out, I interrupted him, telling him how devastated we were and how much we missed him. "We never wanted you to go, and now our hearts are broken."

He told me, "I came to tell you…the last medicine [Norvasc] I took…it killed me. But you have to stay here and take care of the kids and home." He bent down to tie his tennis shoes and said to me, "I have to go. There is a taxi waiting for me."

Tears were racing down my face, choking me. I extended my arms, reaching for him, and I told him, "My heart is broken, and I don't want you to go." I wanted to tell him more, but the words wouldn't come. I said, "One more thing… I bought the space beside you, and I will be buried next to you."

He said, "I know," walked behind the laundry room entrance, and disappeared.

I regretted that neither of us ran to give the other a hug. We just spoke, standing a short distance apart. The moment he disappeared, I woke up distraught but thankful to have seen him one last time and get the answer to my question.

In 2016, I had a dream. I was climbing a big mountain that had a mile of steps to the top. I started my journey and was exhausted by the time I reached the top. At the top of the mountain was Jesus sitting on a wooden chair in front of the dark-brown wooden door. He was in a white robe, wavy light-brown hair down to his shoulders and holding a book in his hands. I took a deep breath from exhaustion and reached the doorknob to open it. He stopped me from trying to open the door. He said, "Wait, you can't go through the door yet. I need to check my book first to see if your name was written in there." He looked through several pages and did not find my name. He told me to go back down the steps to the bottom of the mountain. I did not want to go back down because it was too many steps. He insisted that I have to go back and wait for your name to be written in my book. When I woke up from my dream, I had a question. What was this dream telling me? Did God have a purpose for me and stopped me from seeing the other side of the door? It was not my time.

It was part of my everyday life to wake up before the rising sun and make my way to my prayer spot. Some mornings I'd spend hours there. During the first week of November in 2017, I had an experience during my prayer time. After three minutes of prayer, I saw a yellow light beaming from the icon above the door in my kitchen. It struck my attention like a bolt of lightning. I saw the yellow light as I bowed my head over my prayer book. I couldn't tell which icon it came from. The light went through my whole body. It took me a few seconds to realize this was God answering my prayer. He was sending me peace and comfort. I was scared, and I did not stop praying.

Later in the month, I witnessed another dream. I was sweeping the storage room on the second floor with a straw broom when I came to a little open area to view the floor below. I saw so many beautiful crosses lying on the floor. This brought a smile to my face. I didn't stop to think where they were coming from. I thought, *I love crosses. After all, I have loved them ever since I was a child.*

I sped down the stairs to pick up one of the crosses. I picked it up and turned around to exit the room. Lo and behold, on the red couch with three cushions sat Jesus… He was wearing a beautiful, long white robe that covered his feet. He had wavy brown hair that flowed freely and beautiful brown eyes with a sparkling smile. He stood up and slowly began walking toward me, but I started running to him even faster. I grabbed his arms and kissed his hands, asking him to please, please heal me. I raised my head to look at His face. He gave me a big smile but no words. Still kissing his hands multiple times, his hands slowly disappeared from mine. Then he was gone. He vanished from my view. As I came to, rubbing my eyes and awakening, there was nobody else in the room. Gone. I didn't want that dream to end, nor did I ever want to forget it.

At the end of that week, I had a strong urge to pray. I lit my candle, surrounded by my icons. The candle had almost burned out, then suddenly, the flame jumped high! It was like a strong wind had blown on the candle, sending the flame three times taller. It lasted for a few seconds, then occurred three different times during my prayers.

Candle Miracle during My Morning Prayers

CHAPTER 25

Incident of Prayer Being Answered

A year after losing my darling husband, we held a memorial at our Greek Orthodox Church. I left home on April 23, 2017, with all the food, drinks, and desserts I had prepared for the luncheon. After driving for fifteen minutes, I noticed the car shaking and driving unevenly, as if I was driving over gravel. I pulled to the side of the road to investigate the issue, which turned out to be a shredded tire. I was so upset, knowing that I would be late. I had no idea what to do. I had never changed a tire. I always had my Larry who did those things.

As I circled my car, a tow truck pulled in behind me. A gentleman got out, and I asked, "Who called you? How did you know I had a problem with my car?"

He told me that he happened to be driving behind me and stopped to help.

I called my son to tell him what happened. Ten minutes later, my son was passing by and stopped to help. I made it to church in plenty of time. God knew exactly what will happen on the road that morning and sent the tow truck at the perfect time to help me.

Special prayers were said at the end of the service for my departed husband and his eternal life.

A lady from the church helped me make the traditional *coljivo*, a dish made from wheat, powdered sugar, raisins, white almond candy in the shape of a cross, and chopped parsley. After the luncheon, we visited his resting place.

CHAPTER 26

Life Today

I am thankful for my three beautiful granddaughters, my grandson, and my children Jelena and Alek, who check on me every day. Jelena lives in Warner Robins but expresses her concern daily about me living alone. My son, Alek, works on a Navy base in Jacksonville, Florida, and he still plays soccer for a local team. He calls me every day to hear my voice and asks me how I'm holding up.

While Jelena was never interested in sports, she was always interested in hair and makeup. Upon graduating from high school, she attended Georgia Technical College to become a beautician. I'm so proud of my two amazing children for their accomplishments after all they have endured. They both have successful careers and families of their own. After all these years of separation from their biological father, he now calls to cajole them into sending him money, all the while criticizing them for not staying in contact with him.

My sister, Grozda, in Austria, calls me once a day to let me know she cares about me. She has her own health problems and has survived a heart attack, but she still makes time to talk with me. I have been blessed with such a great support from family.

Each day starts and ends with prayer. I kneel down and thank my heavenly Father for everything he's done for me and my loved ones. This gives me a peace and comfort like none other. As long as I live, I will dedicate my time to Him. The best decision that I ever made was to create my prayer room. My prayer room is my favorite place in my home, where God calls me to spend time with him.

I love my home and never plan to leave it. My husband and I promised each other that it would be our first and last home together. I intend to honor him and keep that promise. I still work at the Cantrell Center, but I cut back to part-time due to health issues and to be able to spend more time with my family and church. I now prepare and eat healthy meals as well as exercise daily. I visit my husband resting place often and wish he were here today to see our grandchildren grow.

I encouraged my family to pray to God every day, no matter the circumstances. He is our security, comfort, and protector. Since I grew up in the Orthodox faith, I was happy to find a Greek Orthodox Church not far from my new American home. When I walk through the doors of the church, I am overwhelmed with joy to find a church that's the same as my church back in Serbia, adorned by beautiful icons. I go weekly and am always welcomed by the friendly people and priest.

I say clearly, no one will ever separate me from my God. These events I write are true. Remembering some of these things are painful. I thought I wouldn't be able to finish this book. But God has pushed me to tell my story and supported me through the journey. Through Him all things are possible. He has assured me that His love always surrounds us.

I have so many reasons to thank the Lord for all blessings received from Him. I know that everything I have lived through wasn't meant to break me but to give me strength for the future. Everything that I endured pushed me to further seek God. After coming to know Him, I have released all my past bitterness, hate, and loneliness. I now know that God's purpose for my life is greater than any of the plans I could have ever made for myself.

I thank him for pulling me out of a dark place and placing me in a beautiful country full of opportunities after years of struggling, God has also blessed me with a wonderful caring family.

I write all these things so that you may seek God in everything that you do and find your purpose as well. I didn't write these events to make you uncomfortable or force my religion on you. But I write to tell you of my encounters with Christ, how He's never forsaken me, and how He will do the same for you. Before He calls me to heaven, I wish to set foot on the land of Kosovo, which is currently under control of the United Nations patrol, where I took my first breath and first step. The land of my people. The resting place of my mom and grandparents.

Please take every opportunity to spend dedicated time alone with God. Pray with all your heart, soul, and mind for His will and thank Him for bringing you thus far. Prayer is personal form of communication where we can speak directly with our father in heaven.

Traditional Orthodox Prayer Room

MILIJANA'S FAVORITE SCRIPTURE

Ask and it will be given to you; seek and you will find; knock and the door will be opened to you.

—Matthew 7:7

Who shall separate us from the love of Christ? Shall trouble or hardship or persecution or famine or nakedness or danger or sword? As it is written: "For your sake we face death all day long; we are considered as sheep to be slaughtered." No, in all these things we are more than conquerors through him who loved us. For I am convinced that neither death nor life, neither angels nor demons, neither the present nor the future, nor any powers, neither height nor depth, nor anything else in all creation, will be able to separate us from the love of God that is in Christ Jesus our LORD.

—Romans 8:35–39

MILIJANA'S FAVORITE PRAYERS

Prayer for times of need: Almighty God, Father of mercy, and God of all consultation, come to my aid and deliver me from all adversity. For I believe, O Lord, that all trials of this life are under Your care and that all things work for the good of those who love You. Take away from me fear, anxiety, and distress. Help me to face and endure my difficulties with faith, courage, and wisdom. Grant that this trial may bring me closer to You. You are my rock and my refuge, my comfort and my hope, my delight and my joy. In Your love and compassion, do I place my trust. For blessed is Your name of the Father, and of the Son, and of the Holy Spirit. Now and forever more. Amen.

Lord Jesus, my God, teach my mind with Your wisdom. That my mouth may always proclaim Your praise. Teach me to reach out to You in my needs. Help me to lead others to You by my example. Amen.

Lord, help me always to remember what is important in my life. No matter what I do or fail to do in my life. Help me always remember the goal of my life is to be with You forever. Remember me in Your kingdom and help me to perfect my faith today and every day. Amen.

Lord, I believe that You created me for a special purpose and that You have a perfect plan for my life. I ask that You fulfill Your purpose for me and help me to do my part by earnestly seeking You daily through prayer on Your word. Thank You that as I seek You each day that You will guide me along the best pathway for my life. In Jesus's name. Amen.

Lord Jesus Christ, our God, hear us from Your holy dwelling place and from the glorious throne of Your kingdom. You are enthroned on high with the Father and are also invisibly present among us. Come and satisfy us and let Your pure body and precious blood be given by Your mighty hand to all Your people. Heavenly Father, give me wisdom with my decisions, help me be efficient with my time. Allow me to glorify You in all the things I do today. Thank You for restoring my soul when it is troubled. Please be with me in the valley of life. Help me not to fear evil. Give me courage during difficult time. Help me stand strong in the face of enemies. Please comfort me when life is hard, and please send Your goodness and mercy to me all the days of my life so that one day I may dwell in Your heavenly kingdom. Amen.

THE ORTHODOX FAITH

The founder of our Orthodox Church is our Lord, Jesus, who was crucified for our remission of sins. Our Orthodox Christian faith is ancient and apostolic. We have a very deep two-thousand-year-old tradition, which has Holy Scripture at its heart. The entirety of our Orthodox Christian tradition has its roots in Christ, the reality of His incarnation, His teachings, and that of His holy apostles. One of the most fundamental parts of our Christian faith and tradition is the reality of the Incarnation. Our Lord and Savior Jesus Christ took on flesh for our salvation. Through this, He bestows upon His blessings and He established His Holy Church, in which the Holy Spirit has dwelled since the Day of Pentecost. We are grafted onto the body of Christ through Holy Baptism. We receive the body and blood of Christ in the Mystery of Holy Communion, just as He instructed. We give glory to God by honoring His Saints who were transfigured in Him. We venerate the Holy Icons as an affirmation of the Incarnation of His taking on and sanctifying matter. And we live out our life in Christ in and through His Holy Church, as Christians have done for the last two thousand years.

ABOUT THE AUTHOR

Milijana Hansee is active in her local Greek Orthodox church. She is a grandmother and enjoys a wonderful life despite the troubles her family endured in Serbia. She wishes to help people understand that in times of trouble, faith in the Lord can help see you through to better days.

She knew in her heart that God wanted her to share this story of her challenges in life. She hopes you will agree that the time is right to share this message of devotion and optimism with the world.

CPSIA information can be obtained
at www.ICGtesting.com
Printed in the USA
LVHW031519180821
695588LV00004B/109